Contemporary Studies in Literature

Eugene Ehrlich, *Columbia University*
Daniel Murphy, *City University of New York*
    Series Editors

Volumes include:

SAMUEL BECKETT, edited by Ruby Cohn

JOSEPH CONRAD, edited by
    Frederick R. Karl

T. S. ELIOT, edited by Linda Wagner

WILLIAM FAULKNER, edited by
    Dean M. Schmitter

F. SCOTT FITZGERALD, edited by
    Kenneth E. Eble

NATHANIEL HAWTHORNE, edited by
    J. Donald Crowley

ERNEST HEMINGWAY, edited by
    Arthur Waldhorn

JAMES JOYCE, edited by
    Chester G. Anderson

FRANZ KAFKA, edited by Leo Hamalian

D. H. LAWRENCE, edited by Leo Hamalian

EZRA POUND, edited by Grace Schulman

MARK TWAIN, edited by Dean M. Schmitter

WALT WHITMAN, edited by Arthur Golden

VIRGINIA WOOLF, edited by
    Thomas S. W. Lewis

W. B. YEATS, edited by Patrick J. Keane

Franz Kafka

a collection of criticism edited by Leo Hamalian

McGraw-Hill Book Company

New York • St. Louis • San Francisco • London • Düsseldorf

Kuala Lumpur • Mexico • Montreal • Panama • São Paulo

Sydney • Toronto • Johannesburg • New Delhi • Singapore

123456789MUMU7987654

Library of Congress Cataloging in Publication Data

Hamalian, Leo, comp.

 Franz Kafka: a collection of criticism.

 (Contemporary studies in literature)
 CONTENTS: Borges, J. L. Kafka and his predecessors.
—Urdazil, J. Kafka's Prague.—Carrouges, M. The
struggle against the father. [etc.]

 1. Kafka, Franz, 1883-1924. I. Title.
PT2621.A26Z74619   833′.9′12   74-10933
ISBN 0-07-025702-7

Contents

91517

Leo Hamalian

Introduction

> *Had one to name the author who comes nearest*
> *to bearing the same kind of relation to our age*
> *as Dante, Shakespeare and Goethe bore to theirs,*
> *Kafka is the first one would think of.* —W. H.
> Auden

An intensely European writer, Franz Kafka has exerted a greater grip on the American consciousness than on the less optimistic European, although his influence on both is by now almost literary legend. This paradox was inevitable. Within the span of their own lifetime, many Europeans experienced firsthand the nightmares best defined by the term his name has given our language: Kafkaesque. Europeans once were sentenced to live in Kafka's kind of walled-in world, a world of trial without error, punishment without crime, and freedom only in fantasies. They came to know the inside of the walls so well that they were loath to experience them again through literature. Their sense of disenchantment with life was so raw, so alive that they could not suffer even a mention of that experience. When fiction approximates reality as closely as Kafka's does, it becomes too faithful, too authentic. It loses its mythopoetic quality of distance. It ceases to be mere fiction and becomes instead an incarnation of a terrifying time and place—something which we might call metafiction. Psychoanalytic theory has it that we can purge ourselves of fear and terror by reliving a bad experience, but this is not always borne out in our lives.

Kafka became something of a vogue among intellectuals and the avant-garde in America shortly after the end of World War II, but those special states of mind conveyed in his writing did not attract a wider audience until the 1950s, that age of anxiety in which the events of the McCarthy era overtook fiction. As Americans began to discover that their mass society had neuroses of its own, they consumed in paper-

1

back and anthology the man who prophesied the ailments of our age. And now, a half-century after his death, the ghost of Kafka challenges us more than ever, and that ominous adjective coined from his name portends the metaphysic of modern America: quietly desperate Josephs and Josephines afflicted by all sorts of insecurity, by nameless threats embedded in everyday life, by unattainable or indefinable spiritual longings; lonely loyal Georges confronted by a possum Authority that is shaking itself and rising again in a rage; penal machinery running amuck; bucket riders facing the prospect of a planet at the end of its energy. We feel inexplicably trapped. On one hand, we fear that no one will prevent a uniformed psychopath from pulling the lever on the engine that spells "Doom," on the other that the Castle itself is empty. We tremble before the possibility that we may be lost forever in the blizzards of disbelief, we suspect that the quester (an American archetype), like K. in *The Castle*, may never reach his destination. Yet are we fascinated by the unfolding of what may be the script for the climax of our own greatest drama. If the future predicted by some ecologists ever should materialize, subsequent generations of readers may regard Kafka as light entertainment. But it would be fatuous of even the most confirmed disciple of progress and democracy not to admit that Kafka's hallucinations are becoming our realities. If we have the feeling of being addressed directly by Kafka, it is because there arises behind all of his questions the great problem of personal freedom, which we Americans thought we had resolved once and for all.

It is, then, experience with the negative elements of our age that Kafka expresses in a variety of forms—novel, story, play, parable, aphorism, and letter—and it is this negative quality that led Communist critics of the forties and fifties to accuse him of wallowing in weakness, self-pity, shallowness, and pessimism. But like all cunning craftsmen, Kafka knew how to transform negation into strength. "A writer sheds his sickness in books—repeats and presents again his emotions to be master of them," wrote D. H. Lawrence. Thomas Mann, referring to those who read the writer, observed appropriately, "They all swear by the name of the great invalid, thanks to those madness they no longer need to be mad." Mad or not, no writer has mirrored the anxieties of being alive for his readers with more candor, wit, and in the end, acceptance than the gangling, sad-faced lawyer who listened during the day to workers' insurance claims and wrote during the evening his original fictions in his modest apartment adjoining the famed cathedral of the Old Town in Prague.

The Prague of the Austro-Hungarian Empire provided the cultural milieu that both spiritually starved and stimulated Kafka. Prague was a city in which tradition and innovation blended and four ethnic strains—

German, Czech, Jewish, Austrian—converged in a continuous flux that should have provided a rich soil in which Kafka's imagination could thrive. Curiously enough, Prague seems to have left less impression on his art than is supposed by Johannes Urdazil (*There Goes Kafka*)[1] and Pavel Eisner (*Franz Kafka and Prague*).[2] Kafka's response to his native city, even to the "spiritual ghetto" where he lived for most of his life, appears to have been largely on the surface (certain landmarks of Prague, for instance, can be identified in his fiction), and the alleged sophistication and warmth of Prague's literary circles of that era seem never to have penetrated the frozen sea deep within the artist. Prague clearly was not to Kafka what Dublin was to Joyce, Paris to Proust, or Mississippi to Faulkner. Kafka's art was forged within the shadows of his private dreams, in the tension created by his white-hot imaginative preoccupation weighed against his disbelief and detachment, in the struggle between his aesthetic commitment and his social isolation. In these terms, almost all his work is spiritual autobiography, an account of the consciousness striving for real contact with the world that a yet deeper impulse insists upon denying.

It was Kafka's loyalty to these challenges that kept him in a state of endless conflict ("neurotic anxiety," some psychologists would say, bringing to mind a Kafka aphorism: "For the last time, psychology!"). Out of that ceaseless conflict came three unfinished novels (*The Trial*, 1925; *The Castle*, 1926; and *Amerika*, 1927), three short novels ("The Metamorphosis," 1915; "The Burrow," c. 1923; and "Investigation of a Dog," 1924), a number of remarkable short stories, prose fragments, fables, an incomplete play, a diary containing not only his daily ruminations but also a scattering of aphorisms which sound like commentaries on his own fiction ("One of the first signs of the beginning of understanding is the wish to die"; "He who seeks does not find, but he who does not seek will be found"), and several collections of revealing letters. While nothing will fully explain the mystery of such creativity, a summary of Kafka's career may cast some light on the conditions that produced the conflicts Kafka converted into art.

Kafka was born in July of 1883, the first among six children, on the edge of Josefstadt, the ghetto of Prague. Zum Turm, the house in which he was born, stood in the Old City on the corner of Maisel and Karpfen Streets, not far from the countless brothels, dives, and junk shops of the area. His father's business prospered, and the family moved to Wenzel Square. This was the first of the repeated changes of residence that marked Kafka's early life. Like Thomas Mann (eight years his senior),

[1] Johannes Urdazil, *There Goes Kafka* (Detroit, Michigan: Wayne State University, 1968).
[2] Pavel Eisner, *Franz Kafka and Prague* (New York: Golden Griffin Books, 1950).

he was the son of a merchant (haberdasher), but Mann's father had gracefully inherited the position of wealth, while Kafka's father had to rise from humble beginnings in a society that despised Jews and regarded them as vermin to be confined in a corner of the city. His success by sheer strength of will turned him into a hardened advocate of external authority—perhaps even a tyrant.

Kafka in childhood also had to endure feelings of alienation in his relations with his three sisters, Elli, Valli, and Ottla, all of whom were born in the more elegant Minuta House on Old City Square, to which the Kafkas had moved in 1889. It was not until later that his warm feelings for Ottla developed. Kafka's father wanted his son to have the kind of education that would facilitate his entry into the German-speaking upper class, and the young Kafka was sent to elementary school in the Masnytrh (Fleischmarkt) and then to the Staromestké (Starpmestle), reputed to be the best German academy in Prague. He had to pass through the Czech world on the way, and he once said to Gustav Janouch *(Conversations with Kafka)*, his much younger admirer: "We walk through the wide avenues of the newly built city, but our steps and glances are unsteady. We still tremble inwardly, as we did in the old little streets of misery."[3]

At the age of fifteen, he began to write, possibly about his sense of rootlessness and apprehension that were connected to his Jewish destiny. We can only conjecture, since he destroyed his juvenilia. He was always to judge his own work severely and to keep destroying things he had written right up to the end of his life.

In 1901, after some hesitation, he decided to study law at the University of Prague and about this time began his friendships with Oscar Pollak, the future historian of baroque art, and with Max Brod, his biographer-to-be. In 1906 he received his doctorate in jurisprudence, and after spending a summer at Triesch with his uncle, Dr. Siegfried Löwy, he entered his uncle Richard Löwy's law office on Old City Square as a clerk, without intending to become a lawyer. Then—for a year—until October 1907, he worked as a clerk at civil and criminal courts without fee, as prescribed for young advocates seeking government positions. For another year he worked in his first job with the Italian insurance firm Assicurazioni-Generali. After he left that company, he worked half-time in a semi-governmental position with the Workmen's Accident Insurance Company. He held that job until 1922, when tuberculosis forced him to resign. In 1910 his superior reported on his work: "Dr. Kafka is an eminent worker and possesses great talent and ambition."

[3] In his *Diaries 1910-1913* Kafka speaks of the "terrible harm" his education caused him, pp. 14-22.

Although this position gave him free afternoons, the sterility of the morning's activities prevented him from pursuing his literary intentions with undeflected energy. Yet Kafka derived a great amount of his knowledge of the world and of life (as well as his skeptical pessimism) from his experiences in the bureaucratic office and from his contact with workmen suffering under the injustices of the system. Entire chapters of his novels and scenes from "In the Penal Colony" contain the elements of absurdity and calmly accepted cruelty in which Kafka found himself immersed every morning at his office. Entries in his *Diary* (started in 1910) reveal how Kafka's imagination was touched by the tragedies of daily existence.

Brief summer vacations meant the opportunity to travel in Europe with his friends, especially with Max Brod, and in 1911 he took many trips—to East Prussia, Switzerland, northern Italy, and Paris. (He had visited northern Italy and Paris previously in the company of Brod.) Even in Prague, where he struggled to maintain a schedule of work, sleep, and writing, he associated with other intellectuals of his time—the theologian Martin Buber, the novelist Franz Werfel, the writer Oscar Bau, Professor Friedl Pick, and members of the Bar-Kochba circle. By now two sections from "Description of a Struggle" had been published in Franz Blei's journal *Hyperion* (1910), probably Kafka's first appearance in print, and Max Brod had been writing about him in the Berlin weekly *Die Gegenwart*. Approaching the age of thirty, Kafka felt himself ready to write seriously. By 1913, he was working on three stories, "The Judgment," "The Metamorphosis," and "The Boy Who Was Never More Heard of," the first sketch of the work published posthumously as *Amerika*.

During the previous summer, while vacationing in the Harz Mountains, Kafka had met Felice Bauer (F.B.), "the girl from Berlin." For the next five years Kafka vacillated between the wish to marry F.B. (or at least maintain the love relationship that had been sealed by an engagement in 1914) and the desire to devote his energies to his literary work. He could not, apparently, do both and he decided to resign himself to isolation in order to preserve his creative self. When he was later afflicted by tuberculosis, he felt a great sense of relief: it was God or some force beyond himself, he reasoned, that made him incapable of loving, friendship, or profession.

Despite uncertain health, Kafka in 1914 was undertaking trips to the north of Germany, where he may have met "a certain lady M.M." They had a brief affair, and M.M. bore Kafka a child who died at the age of seven in Munich. Max Brod says that the tragedy of this situation was that Kafka had not even an inkling of the existence of the boy. The effect on Kafka, had he learned that he was the father of a son, would have been enormous, Brod believes, exercising a beneficent influence on his development. Instead there was the stimulation of his strengthening friendship with Franz Werfel. Kafka began to write *The Trial* and "In the Penal Colony." Both works have been interpreted on many levels—political, social, psychological, theological, and even autobiographical. (A Kafka aphorism links bachelorhood with the act of slow suicide.) Both open with a crisis in the life of a man who has recognized the abyss of absurdity lying before him. In the short story, an explorer who comes to the island of the execution machine, and in *The Trial*, Joseph K. (whose family name must be Karl, from the maternal uncle so identified in the novel), must infuse meaning into an existence that may be inherently meaningless. Fixated on this question, Joseph K. falls "under arrest." Is it an actual arrest? Is he criminally guilty? If so, of what? These are the questions Peter Webster seeks to answer in his brilliant psychological study called "'Dies Irae' in the Unconscious, or the Significance of Franz Kafka." Or is Joseph K. guiltlessly guilty, a victim of his own existence who must, like Job, suffer punishment without having committed a discernible crime? Two years later, when World War I, the most senseless of all wars, erupted, many Europeans would feel like Joseph K.[4]

Like Thomas Mann and D. H. Lawrence, Kafka did not participate in the fighting. His position as a civil servant granted him exemption from military duty and allowed him the freedom to travel within Hungary, even to stay for a while at Marienbad with F.B. During the war years, he wrote his powerful "Aphorisms" and that surreal masterpiece called "A Country Doctor," which is composed of a single driving paragraph about a physician who answers a call in the night and ends up lost in a blizzard. He finished "The Bucket Rider," a little gem of a story that reflects, among other issues, the fuel crisis that distressed war-time Prague, and began to write the long narrative, "The Great Wall of China." After moving to a new residence in Prague (Ulicka), Kafka took the occasion to unburden himself of his feelings toward his father in the famous letter he gave to his mother but never to his father. This letter provides overwhelming proof that "the unbreathable atmosphere of Kafka's tales is not, then, a gratuitous invention of his imagination; his art flows out of the conflict with his father" (*Kafka versus Kafka*). As further evidence of the violent feeling that underlay the father-son relationship, we have "The Judgment" and "The Metamorphosis," stories in which a son is destroyed by a father's fury. With characteristic gentleness, Kafka once told his friend Gustav Janouch, when speaking

---

[4] A quarter of a century later, on the eve of another world conflict, a French-Algerian writer named Albert Camus grappled with the same question in a novel called *The Stranger*.

of his father, "Love often wears the face of violence," a profound observation that throws open an entirely new approach to Kafka's stories.

Kafka suffered his first attack of tuberculosis in 1917, spitting up blood shortly after a final break with F.B. (Tuberculosis briefly touched Thomas Mann and caused the death of D. H. Lawrence.) Kafka took sick leave from his job and launched himself into the study of Hebrew and the philosophy of Sören Kierkegaard (*Sickness Unto Death; In Fear and Trembling*). This growing concern with religious mysticism coincided with the first attack of tuberculosis and the break with F.B. Three years later, his condition required treatment in the mountains of northern Italy and, the following winter, confinement to a sanatorium in the Tatra Mountains. About this time he began an affair with Milena Jesenská, an unhappily married Czech writer who had translated some of his work. We are fortunate to have a description of the affair in *Letters to Milena*, an extraordinary document that divulges one of Kafka's demons—touching, horrifying, brilliant, sickening, heartbreaking, and infinitely convoluted. Again Kafka was to deny love for the labor of love: "What I have to do, I can only do alone. Become clear about ultimate things: the Western Jew is not clear about them and therefore has no right to marry." While involved in this hopeless affair, he was engaged in writing the first draft of a never quite completed novel, *The Castle* (first translated in 1930). The hero, a land surveyor called K., apparently is summoned to a village that is overlooked and overlorded by "the Castle," where he is to get his instructions. The entire novel consists of K.'s attempts to enter this mysterious edifice and to get his instructions. After reading *Letters to Milena*, one reads *The Castle* with fresh insight, since so many lines, notions, and situations flash the reader back to the letters. And possibly Kafka, in writing that enigmatic novel, approached the ultimate clarity that he had despaired, in the letters, of ever knowing: Ultimate clarity is unknowable and unreachable no matter how determined the quest for certainty. For an unorthodox interpretation of this novel, the reader should turn to Erwin Steinberg's "K. of *The Castle*: Ostensible Land-Surveyor."

Kafka once had written in his diary that the only one who could wholly understand him was God, but he discovered near the end of his life that he might have been mistaken. In 1923, while staying with his sister and her children at the Baltic resort of Muritz, he met and fell deeply in love with Dora Dymant, a twenty-year-old orthodox Polish Jew employed by the Berlin Jewish People's Home there. He returned to Prague from his holiday full of high courage and resolved to cut all ties, go to Berlin, and live with Dora. When Max Brod visited the couple in the suburb of Steglitz, he "found an idyll." Living in these happy circumstances, Kafka wrote some of his finest stories: "A Little Woman,"

"The Burrow," "Josephine the Singer," "Investigations of a Dog," and "A Hunger Artist," a story somewhat reminiscent of "The Metamorphosis," with the horror and violence muted, and the Jewish humor about the son who refuses to eat exploited effectively.

Kafka lived in Berlin until the spring of 1924, when his rapidly failing health forced him to depart, accompanied by his faithful Dora, for the Wiener wald Sanatorium. He wrote from there to Dora's father, asking for permission to marry his daughter. The father, after consulting a rabbi, refused to give his consent. After a short time at a clinic in Vienna, Kafka was moved to a sanatorium in Kierling, near Vienna. On June 3, not far from the home where Beethoven created some of his most memorable music, Kafka went into a coma from which he never recovered, with Dora Dymant and his friend Robert Klopstock at his bedside. He is buried in the Löwy corner of the cemetery behind the Straschnitz Synagogue in Prague, where the names of his sisters are carved into the brick wall of a memorial to the victims of the Nazi concentration camps. A niece (Ottla's daughter), an engaging woman named Vera Saudkova, works for a publishing house in Prague. Another niece lives in London. They are the only members of the family to survive the holocaust.

* * *

Appearing at this point, fifty years after his death, a collection of Kafka criticism must at least correct the excesses of the earlier interpretations, which served the purpose of arousing interest in his work and extending his reading public. (These excesses are described in H. S. Reiss' *German Life and Letters*.) Too often Kafka was judged by critics bent on subordinating the events and mood of his work to their own preoccupations, from metaphysics to Marxist dialectics. Though the nonliterary approaches may yield certain valid insights (after all, the writer's work does have a content or a *significance* apart from the *signification—vide* Roland Barthes' essay), on the whole they have damaged Kafka's reputation and have made his work the happy hunting-grounds of the eccentric, the bizarre, or the overly ingenious mind. It has been argued that Kafka's work encourages such speculation. The answer, of course, is that criticism which begins with special premises ends up ignoring the artist's intention and, at its worst, the work itself.

With his reputation secure, he no longer needs the attention of special interests. In this anthology, some critics take a particular approach, but almost all keep the text primarily and steadily in view, so that the tail does not wag the dog. These critics do not use his work as a literary Rorschach test. They focus on the text with a magnifying glass, examining the images, the metaphors, the events, the language itself that combine to create the fabric of an apparently simple Kafka fable. The writers who have found inspiration in Kafka—Borges, Barthes, Auden, and West—seek the essence of the man, so that the careful textual analysis is balanced by a broader vision of the total man. In each of these essays, the reader is made aware that Kafka was an artist, not a philosopher or metaphysician.

What do we mean when we say that a man is an "artist"? We mean several things, but most important, that his vision exposes us to different and new ways of seeing and feeling, thereby opening up in us the possibility of extending the range of our own sentient life. In "Kafka's Precursors," the great Argentinian writer Jorge Borges (for whom Kafka was a precursor) proposes that Kafka's work creates for us new emotional states. These states we may have encountered before in the work of other writers, but we did not recognize them until Kafka described them with his particular kind of precision. Thus, Zeno's paradox of the moving arrow that can never reach its destination is a key to *The Castle*; Robert Browning's poem about a man who believes he has a famous friend although he has never seen him appears to prefigure "The Judgment"; Leon Bloy's story about some people who travel only in their minds, without ever leaving their homes, and Lord Dunsany's story about an army that travels but never reaches its destination foretell the themes of the three novels; and Kierkegaard's religious parables on contemporary and bourgeois themes gain in meaning after we have read Kafka. As Borges suggests, our reading of Kafka "sharpens and deflects" our reading of these earlier writers; through the looking glass of his work, we receive a fresh view of his precursors. And just as his work modifies our conception of the past, "it will modify the future" (Borges himself being a case in point).

In the next selection, Johannes Urdazil in "Kafka's Prague" recalls the cultural and social milieu of the Czech capital in which Kafka passed most of his life. These recollections are from the point of view of a one-sided concentration, to compensate for that other one-sided perspective to which almost the whole body of Kafka criticism is committed. "We are the air we breathe," writes Robert Penn Warren, and Urdazil is undeniably valuable to us because he himself shared the air that Kafka breathed. But Borges, in the preceding piece, warns us against falling into any simple or easy interpretation of what it is that constitutes that atmosphere.

Something similar may be said about Michel Carrouges' "The Struggle Against the Father." It is important to know about the nature of Kafka's relationship with his father so long as we do not insist on interpreting all Kafka in this light—a reductive process that has been the curse of Kafka criticism. In reaction to this naive approach, one would be tempted to assert that the famous letter to his father is nothing more than a cunning piece of invention, like "The Judgment" or "The Metamorphosis," were it not for the wind of terror that blows through it so consistently. Carrouges' essay breaks no fresh ground, but its temperate and balanced analysis of the letter as a key, as an autobiographical document, lends his argument the discipline so often missing in other criticism that sees as central to Kafka's work his neurotic relationship with his father. Carrouges regards the relationship as tragic, even though Kafka converted the unequal struggle into art.

In "The I Without a Self," W. H. Auden identifies the absurdist character of Kafka's work which has affinities with his own writing. H. S. Reiss, a Canadian critic of Kafka, says that Auden insists too much on the metaphysical quality of Kafka, but he fails to notice the excellent key that Auden's essay provides for understanding the dominant archetype of the later Kafka stories. They are developed around a radical revision of the traditional quest narrative. Kafka takes this formula and turns it upside down until it illustrates his own aphorism, "There is a goal but no way." The hero is uncertain about his purpose, hemmed in by a suffocating world, blocked at every step of his negative quest. Even the thought of finding freedom is given an absurd twist: Is it possible, after all, that imprisonment is the natural state of human kind? That the idea of freedom is nothing but a fantasy? "We think of the key, each in his prison/Thinking of the key, each confirms a prison," goes a pair of lines in *The Waste Land*, leading us to believe that Kafka was among the writers that Eliot raided.

In "Kafka's Answer," Roland Barthes, the author of a slim but influential volume of criticism, *Writing Degree Zero*, develops Camus' statement that Kafka offers everything but confirms nothing.[5] The bureaucratic terror of the modern moment, the subjugation of the individual, solitude, alienation, quest, absurdity—these are themes that belong to all literature rather than to Kafka alone, nor do they distinguish his work from other writers'. Barthes claims that Kafka should not be equated with Kafka-ism, which "has nourished the most contrary literatures, from Camus to Ionesco." His meaning is not to be understood in terms of sources and ideas, nor is it woven of symbols, whose meanings must be agreed upon if they are to have significance.

---

[5] In "Hope and the Absurd in the Work of Franz Kafka," from *The Myth of Sisyphus*, Camus elevates Kafka into a protagonist of the existential philosophy of Absurdity. The essay has the cogency of thought and the urgency of feeling that characterize Camus' expository writing, but it is essentially a suite of aphoristic paragraphs, not unlike its companion novel, *The Stranger*, in its (deliberate?) lack of coherence and unity.

Kafka must be grasped through his *technique*, through his system of signs rather than what is signified by the signs. Kafka strips the implied "as if" out of metaphor so that the events and characters become the metaphor translated literally into the world. Gregor is not "like a cockroach" and neither does his state "symbolize" anything—he *is*, simply, a cockroach. By forcing a literal level of being on us, the Kafka narrative authorizes many equally plausible explanations without validating any of them—or intending to validate them. Kafka's language possesses the same tentative, undefined quality of phenomena themselves and, through this quality of evasiveness, resembles and even asserts the world, though it tends to be interrogative rather than assertive. Not all the critics assembled in this volume would accept that position, although commentators on Kafka are increasingly loath to assign specific meanings to the people, events, and atmosphere of his cryptic creations.[6]

"The Judgment," written in one powerful overnight burst of energy, is Kafka's first complete story. As the essay by Michel Carrouges indicates, Kafka's fear of his father (about which Kafka was so astonishingly clear-sighted that we must wonder whether he did not succeed in self-analyzing it away) throws useful light on this story, but for a fuller understanding of it we must go beyond biographical background. Kierkegaard seems to have exerted a strategic influence on Kafka's own developing view of the world. In reading Kierkegaard, says Anthony Thorlby in his essay, Kafka recognized how deeply the Danish philosopher touched upon his own condition—especially in his Concept of Dread, that experience evoked in many people by an awareness of selfhood and of the infinite discrepancy between what we know and what we are. When he turned to writing, Kafka was able to translate to the realm of fiction his reactions to what the psychiatrist Victor Frankl has defined as "the existential vacuum." This abyss of uncertainty Kafka approached from a background quite unlike Kierkegaard's, but he was similarly convinced that this "sense of Nothingness" springs from a confrontation between self-conscious intelligence and the tremendous mystery of temporal existence.[7] Thus, "The Judgment" (says Thorlby) conveys the critical experience of Dread. But the story must be under-

---

[6] Gunther Anders, in "The Literal Metaphor," from his book, *Kafka,* makes much the same point as Barthes, that Kafka's stories are neither allegorical nor symbolic, but revive some "forgotten visual or literal significance in a word or phrase. By illuminating the detail inherent in an image, he makes language yield a new insight into the reality of our world." After reading Kafka, W. H. Auden said the same thing about his own poetry.

[7] The theme of human suffering and loss of confidence in living brought about by consciousness is a major theme of Dostoevski's *Notes from Underground.* Lionel Trilling, in "The Fate of Pleasure," from *Beyond Culture*, believes that Dostoevski (and therefore Kafka?) affirms unlife as the highest form of life.

stood as a totally "inner" encounter. The characters, for instance, must be interpreted as modalities within Kafka's mind, as "projections of different aspects of his psyche," not as real people or as anything outside of it. Whatever his actual father (and fiancée and friend) may have meant to him in actual life (businessman, potential mate, bourgeois moral code, Jewish belief), in the story itself the events and characters reflect only Kafka's private *relationship* to these things: his relationship to the "sources of his own life, to the inscrutable and frightening fact of being alive, which he—like the rest of us—tried to cover up in conventional platitudes, pretending it was normal when deep down he knew it was monstrous and absurd."[8] It was in this mood that Kafka created his next work.

Perhaps the best-known story of Kafka—some critics say his masterpiece—is "The Metamorphosis." I have given it the spacious coverage of Martin Greenberg's "Gregor Samsa and Modern Spirituality," from his admirable study, *The Terror of Art: Kafka and Modern Literature*. In this book, Greenberg describes and defines what he believes to be Kafka's favorite form, "the dream narrative," tracing its evolution from its beginnings to its culmination in *The Castle.*[9] The "dream narrative" became for Kafka the appropriate form for revealing a world wherein reason, consciousness, conscience, and suffering no longer serve the Self to find the true way, but operate as means by which an oppressive world rules for its own ends. At the end of the dream, Gregor Samsa's remains are swept away like so much garbage. Kafka said to his friend Janouch: "The dream reveals the reality, which conception lags behind. This is the horror of Life—the terror of art." The consciousness that conceives lags behind, seeks to stifle knowledge of the reality which is known unconsciously and which is revealed in dream work. The horror of life, which puts us on trial, is the fact that the self is split in this way rather than being whole, so we do not know who we are or what we do. In Greenberg's words, "The dream-narrative form made it possible for the

---

[8] Thorlby's view both refines and expands one of Camus' ideas, but ultimately differs from it. Camus says that Kafka's work is not truly Absurd, but "universal because its inspiration is religious. As in all religions, man is freed of the weight of his own life"—an oblique comment on Georg Bendemann of "The Judgement."

[9] Bernard Groethuysen, in his preface to the French edition of *The Trial,* follows the fancies of what he calls "a daydreamer." This, of course, is not what Greenberg has in mind. In Calvin Hall and Richard Lind, *Dreams, Life, and Literature,* the authors analyze, with the aid of a computer, Kafka's dreams as he reported them in his diaries and his *Letters to Milena*—thirty-seven dreams in all, over a period of 13 years. The data leading to their conclusions are worth looking at for the reader interested in speculating about Kafka's inner life; for one interested in his work, they are valuable only if continuity can be established between his life and his work. The authors have a hard time demonstrating that such a relationship holds true.

imagination to plumb depths of the self which were otherwise out of reach. The inward, introspective, visionary characteristic of modern literature is carried by Kafka to a very far point indeed. With him, literature gropes to the very bottom of the mind, seeking the unconscious self in its very condition of hiddenness, in all its turbidity and strickenness." For Freud, the dream was distortion, an attempt to disguise the very wish the dream tries to satisfy. The dream was a kind of psychic delinquency, a subvention of the law. For Kafka the dream was the opposite of "dishonest"—it is the inner self in fear and trembling telling the truth and creating out of that truth—within the dream, Gregor Samsa awakens from a dream and discovers that he has been banished from his family and from the world of humanity. "The Metamorphosis" is a perfect illustration of Kafka's art of elaborating, unfolding the basic image. Typical of his work, this story is *visionary* rather than *dramatic*: it does not follow the familiar progression of beginning, middle, and end, but moves through *intensities of seeing*, toward an even deeper, more disturbing vision. Nothing happens in the story that is not predicated in that opening sentence, intended (as Kafka put it in one of his letters) to make us "suffer like the death of someone we love more than ourselves." Kafka's world coincides with the truth of the dream—in "The Metamorphosis," the dream of one's own death. In our dreams we know there is no hereafter, no paradise to be regained, no separation between sickness and health, no boundaries such as the waking ego creates. Kafka knew that we have been expelled permanently from Grace, and Gregor Samsa, possessing that knowledge, dies of spiritual starvation, of his own will. In this respect, Greenberg points out, the story is different from the earlier tale, "The Judgment," in which the son accepts the verdict of death from his father. The story, finally, is about dehumanization—even the unemotional style suggests this significance.

"In the Penal Colony," after "The Metamorphosis" the longest short story Kafka wrote during his most productive years, is also about dehumanization, but Heinz Politzer's study, "Parable and Paradox: 'In the Penal Colony'" examines the complementary relationship between that story and *The Trial*. The two are parallel in their conception of the "paradoxical nature of law"; they are, however, "sharply distinguished from one another by the fact that K's guilt in *The Trial* remains unknown, whereas the soldier's offense . . . is more than clearly stated." Again, the execution machine is the mystery of the law, but the Commandant's law is founded on a logic outside the pattern of civilized justice. It seems to be primitive, but is actually inexorable—guilt is never to be doubted. Everyone is guilty of everything. There are other interfaces: the law court of *The Trial* becomes embodied in the figure of the officer—judge, jailer, and hangman. The verdict of the machine corresponds to the door in the parable called "Before the Law" in *The Trial*. When the outsider pronounces judgment upon the machine and the law it represents, the officer commits suicide. (Does this represent a reversal of the plot in "The Judgment"?) His death and the breakdown of the machine, which Politzer sees as a symbol of technological dehumanization combined with "the barbarous primitiveness of a divinely justified martial law," appear to be a piece of optimism until we remember the prophecy that the island will be recaptured, the old Commandant will return, and the torture machine will again imprint the victim's offense on his body strapped to the Bed. This, Politzer concludes, is Kafka's vision of a Second Coming.

Like Martin Greenberg, Walter Sokel in "On 'The Country Doctor'" thinks that the enigmatic suggestiveness of the typical Kafka narrative comes from its striking resemblance to dreams. Different from the writings of the dream-directed surrealists, his stories are by contrast "thoroughly disciplined," and as in dreams, they take the metaphors buried in words and enact them—an observation that Roland Barthes makes in his essay. Sokel takes one of the most mystifying and puzzling of Kafka's stories, "The Country Doctor," and by applying these premises makes it intelligible to the mind as well as to the emotions. The story dramatizes the dream of the divided self. It is a dream which can come to the surface only if it wears disguises. The groom who rapes Rose and the physician who answers the call for help are the two opposing forces in the psyche of the doctor, locked in deadly conflict. The rapist lives in the pigsty which the doctor himself opens. He is the forgotten dweller of the lower depths. Thus the metaphor is reactivated and realized in the events of the narrative. By connecting organically the enactment of one metaphor with the enactment of others, Kafka establishes narrative development. By examining the interconnected images (not the isolated images), Sokel believes we will recognize pictorial translations of overriding personal concerns in Kafka's own life, which through the craft of his art he endowed with universal significance.

Hermann J. Weigand, in "Franz Kafka's 'The Burrow' ('Der Bau'): An Analytical Essay," gives us the definitive study of what was probably the last story that Kafka wrote. Previous commentators have emphasized the correlation between those motifs and problems that recur obsessively in his work and have disclosed the "intimate relation, often amounting to identity, between the author and the persona of the story" (which Weigand does not deny). Though this approach has led to a number of stimulating insights (as well as mistaken readings) on various levels of symbolic interpretation, Weigand's close scrutiny of the story on the primary level, while long and intricate, proves to be far more coherent and fruitful. The unique quality of "The Burrow," Weigand is able to demonstrate, depends upon the synchronous flow of two realities, separate yet fused: there is the ninety-minute monologue in the emergent or progressive present, co-existing with a past life that spans many years, from maturity to approaching senility (again, the reader is reminded of Samuel Beckett, especially of the novels and of *Krapp's Last Tape*). The mind of the narrator undergoes a gradual deterioration during the recital until it reaches the point of derangement; in the process of breakdown and self-exposure, his persecution mania reveals a repressed, abnormal libido that strongly suggests some unnamed, shameful traumatic experience in his youth.[10] And his ruminations about the "relentless approach of a silent predator"—are they grounded in reality or are they figments of his imagination? On this crucial issue, Weigand's view is radical but persuasive, and the reader, I hope, will enjoy the intellectual exhilaration of watching it develop. At the end of his essay, using some clues in the text, Weigand envisions a possible ending for the story, ingenious and inventive, but since Kafka nowhere even hints that he would sanction this interpretation, Weigand accepts the ambiguity of Kafka's conclusion as final and as artistically accurate.[11]

Even though Dame Rebecca West's interpretation of *The Trial* and *The Castle* has to an extent been assimilated by more recent Kafka criticism, it would be a lamentable error of omission if one of the keenest intellects and most graceful writers of English prose were not represented in this book. Dame Rebecca warns the reader not to take either of these novels as exercises in fantasy. They are rooted in the reality of the bureaucratic institutions that Kafka knew more intimately than most people. He set down what he knew in a completely objective way, and if they strain belief, it is only because the reality itself is fantastic, not the imagining of the narrator. Both novels slyly mock the Hapsburg law that Jews had to respect as the law of the land even though it was

[10] Ruth Tiefenbrun, in *Moment of Terror*, pp. 3 and 11, writes: "Although Kafka always told the truth, it was seldom the whole truth. He always withheld at least one key fact in order to guard his secret . . . which was later reflected in the anguish of all his major characters." This secret, Ms. Tiefenbrun contends, was his homosexuality, and although she does not discuss "The Burrow" in her book, we can invent *à la* Roth and Weigand, some authentic lines for her: "When one reads the totality of Kafka's writings, it becomes apparent that the predicament of all his heroes and the unnamed traumatic experience of the burrower are based on the fact that they are all homosexuals. If we accept this thesis, all of Kafka's incomprehensible stories become quite meaningful and the burrower's love of holes becomes intelligible."

[11] Previous critics have regarded the story as an unfinished fragment. Weigand, of course, disagrees with this view.

hostile to them. No rebel, Kafka figured out a strategy for conforming to the conflicting laws of both the dominant power and of his own people.

Thus, while both novels are basically satires on the Hapsburg bureaucracy, which Kafka regarded as beneficent, comic, murderous, cruel, and absolutely necessary, there are also religious allegories beneath the realistic surface. In West's words, Joseph K. is a "soul laboring under the conviction that he has sinned against God," and K. is a "soul anxious to serve God but who cannot find out what it is that God wills him to do." In both allegories, the protagonists wish to see the face of God, but God does not appear. If we accept this analysis, we have in Kafka the seeds of Beckett's *Waiting for Godot*.

Somewhere in Kierkegaard is the story about the absent-minded man who was so abstracted from life that he did not know he existed until one morning when he woke up to find himself dead. Joseph K., according to Peter Webster in "'Dies Irae' in the Unconscious, or the Significance of Franz Kafka," is such a man, one who in middle life wakes up to discover that he has not touched the roots of his existence. The psychologist's perfect dreamer, Kafka in *The Trial* has written an allegory about the judgment of the Consciousness by the Unconsciousness. The Unconsciousness accuses, tries, and condemns the Consciousness, thus reversing the assumption that the ego is a free agent in relating to reality. Because Joseph K. has lived without warmth, without contact or engagement with the life of feeling or the underground forces of the psyche, the Unconsciousness sends out emissaries to "arrest" him. In this kind of situation, no one is ever entirely free because the Unconsciousness is always there even though repressed. If one adjusts to the situation and faces it, he may get ostensible acquittal or postponement. Once on trial, Joseph K. is advised, "throw yourself on the court's mercy"—why? The Unconsciousness is always right—in the court of the Unconscious, there are no errors. The absurdity of the arrest and the following events result from Joseph K.'s failure to bring the world of ego and id into line. Like Heinz Politzer, Peter Webster tends to picture Kafka pitted against Kafka in a drama of "the divided self," even though they assign opposite values to the representative of the underground. Webster sometimes descends into sheer silliness, but his reading has the virtue of making the novel seem coherent where other interpretations render the verdict of "irrational" on this most rational of books.

If Freud may be the key to *The Trial*, then fraud may be the key to *The Castle*—this latter possibility forms the crux of Erwin Steinberg's "K. of *The Castle*: Ostensible Land-Surveyor." Many critics (like Dame

Rebecca West) have assumed that *The Castle* is the story of man's attempt to reach salvation, religious or otherwise. Steinberg argues that, to the contrary, K. is seeking a salvation that he has neither been awarded nor earned, and that indeed his identity as a land-surveyor is questionable. He is making demands that he has no right to make. If this is Kafka's view of man's journey through life or his relationship to God, Steinberg says, then it is even more bitter than critics have been led to believe: not only will man not achieve salvation, but he is presumptuous even to think of seeking it. Seen in this perspective, the mood comes close to Samuel Beckett's bleak vision of life. Readers will have to reread the novel carefully before they can challenge this ingenious piece of skepticism.

Klaus Mann's essay appeared originally as the preface to the Muir translation of *Amerika*. For Kafka, Prague was both paradise and prison, and the most extensive journey he ever made away from it, Mann maintains, took place wholly in his mind, to the United States. Although as a whole his picture of America has poetical truth, his whole Czech geography, his sense of guilt follow Karl Rossman to America, and the great trial continues amid the endless highways of America. Karl is hero, victim, sinner, martyr, and clown in his own miracle play, which Kafka suggested enigmatically to his friends was to have a happy ending. It is the only one of the three novels, Mann points out, in which a confident mood prevails—Karl (Kafka?) becomes an individual unfettered from the claims of clan, family, tradition, religion, or country. Did Kafka sense that Europe was coming to an end, that only America promised the possibility of a future? Did America hold out the promise of escape?

Before leaving the subject of Kafka and America, it is inevitable that we ask whether his work has influenced American writers. In *The New Novel in America,* Helen Weinberg examines "the impress of the Kafkan hero on the minds of the American writers who, from the internal evidence of their work, demonstrate that they share his sensibility." These writers—Saul Bellow, Norman Mailer, Bernard Malamud, William Styron, J. D. Salinger, and Philip Roth—have "transformed the Kafkan vision by using it in a way that coincides with American consciousness and with their own native perceptions." That vision, the editor of this collection hopes, is made more visible by these essays.

Jorge Luis Borges

Kafka and His Precursors[1]

I once premeditated making a study of Kafka's precursors. At first I had considered him to be as singular as the phoenix of rhetorical praise; after frequenting his pages a bit, I came to think I could recognize his voice, or his practices, in texts from diverse literatures and periods. I shall record a few of these here, in chronological order.

The first is Zeno's paradox against movement. A moving object at A (declares Aristotle) cannot reach point B, because it must first cover half the distance between the two points, and before that, half of the half, and before that, half of the half of the half, and so on to infinity; the form of this illustrious problem is, exactly, that of *The Castle*, and the moving object and the arrow and Achilles are the first Kafkian characters in literature. In the second text which chance laid before me, the affinity is not one of form but one of tone. It is an apologue of Han Yu, a prose writer of the ninth century, and is reproduced in Margoulie's' admirable *Anthologie raisonée de la littérature chinoise* (1948). This is the paragraph, mysterious and calm, which I marked: "It is universally admitted that the unicorn is a supernatural being of good omen; such is declared in all the odes, annals, biographies of illustrious men and other texts whose authority is unquestionable. Even children and village women know that the unicorn constitutes a favorable presage. But this animal does not figure among the domestic beasts, it is not always easy to find, it does not lend itself to classification. It is not like the horse or the bull, the wolf or the deer. In such conditions, we could be face to face with a unicorn and not know for certain what it was. We know that such and such an animal with a mane is a horse and that such and

[1] Translated by J.E.I.

such an animal with horns is a bull. But we do not know what the unicorn is like."[2]

The third text derives from a more easily predictable source: the
writings of Kierkegaard. The spiritual affinity of both writers is something of which no one is ignorant; what has not yet been brought out,
as far as I know, is the fact that Kierkegaard, like Kafka, wrote many
religious parables on contemporary and bourgeois themes. Lowrie, in
his *Kierkegaard* (Oxford University Press, 1938), transcribes two of
these. One is the story of a counterfeiter who, under constant surveil-
lance, counts banknotes in the Bank of England; in the same way, God
would distrust Kierkegaard and have given him a task to perform, precisely because He knew that he was familiar with evil. The subject of
the other parable is the North Pole expeditions. Danish ministers had
declared from their pulpits that participation in these expeditions was
beneficial to the soul's eternal well-being. They admitted, however, that
it was difficult, and perhaps impossible, to reach the Pole and that not
all men could undertake the adventure. Finally, they would announce
that any trip—from Denmark to London, let us say, on the regularly
scheduled steamer—was, properly considered, an expedition to the North
Pole. The fourth of these prefigurations I have found is Browning's
poem "Fears and Scruples," published in 1876. A man has, or believes
he has, a famous friend. He has never seen this friend and the fact is
that the friend has so far never helped him, although tales are told of
his most noble traits and authentic letters of his circulate about. Then
someone places these traits in doubt and the handwriting experts de-
clare that the letters are apocryphal. The man asks, in the last line:
"And if this friend were . . . God?"

My notes also register two stories. One is from Léon Bloy's *Histoires
désobligeantes* and relates the case of some people who possess all manner of globes, atlases, railroad guides and trunks, but who die without
ever having managed to leave their home town. The other is entitled
"Carcassonne" and is the work of Lord Dunsany. An invincible army of
warriors leaves an infinite castle, conquers kingdoms and sees monsters
and exhausts the deserts and the mountains, but they never reach
Carcassonne, though once they glimpse it from afar. (This story is, as
one can easily see, the strict reverse of the previous one; in the first, the
city is never left; in the second, it is never reached.)

If I am not mistaken, the heterogeneous pieces I have enumerated

---

[2] Nonrecognition of the sacred animal and its opprobrious or accidental death at
the hands of the people are traditional themes in Chinese literature. See the last
chapter of Jung's *Psychologie und Alchemie* (Zürich, 1944), which contains two
curious illustrations.

resemble Kafka; if I am not mistaken, not all of them resemble each other. This second fact is the more significant. In each of these texts we find Kafka's idiosyncrasy to a greater or lesser degree, but if Kafka had never written a line, we would not perceive this quality; in other words, it would not exist. The poem "Fears and Scruples" by Browning foretells Kafka's work, but our reading of Kafka perceptibly sharpens and deflects our reading of the poem. Browning did not read it as we do now. In the critics' vocabulary, the word "precursor" is indispensable, but it should be cleansed of all connotation of polemics or rivalry. The fact is that every writer *creates* his own precursors. His work modifies our conception of the past, as it will modify the future.[3] In this correlation the identity or plurality of the men involved is unimportant. The early Kafka of *Betrachtung* is less a precursor of the Kafka of somber myths and atrocious institutions than is Browning or Lord Dunsany.

[3] See T. S. Eliot: *Points of View* (1941), pp. 25-26.

Johannes Urzidil

Kafka's Prague

How did it come about that in the first and second decades of this century German literature could flourish in Prague, of all places, with so much power and originality? What aggregate of vital forces played a part in this creative and literary milieu? I ought to know the answers because I was born and grew up there, and I was a witness as well as a participant in that German intellectual world of Prague, full of universal ideas, ever new forms, and ethical enthusiasms. But a quick and unambiguous judgment about the reasons for this phenomenon is impossible. Furthermore, the social, biological, and other assumptions rooted in the material universe can be useful only in part. Such a phenomenon as the congregation of a startlingly large number of significant creative personalities, frequently of the highest rank, within a relatively short period of time and within the narrow confines of a city (just as earlier in Weimar or in Concord) must always remain something sublime and metaphysical. Most of the German authors in Prague were Jews, but their feelings as members of a minority group emerged only on occasion. Their German-language consciousness determined their sense of history more strongly than their descent was ever able to do: (I am using concepts here which were compellingly adduced by the Prague philosopher Felix Weltsch in his study of Kafka). My approach may enjoy a certain corroboration, however incomplete, by virtue of the notion of structure or structural quality *(Gestaltsqualität),* an idea conclusively developed by my teacher Christian, Baron of Ehrenfels and later by Max Wertheimer of Prague. This idea more than anything else provides an ability to recognize the secret of a literary physiognomy, whose disparate

Reprinted from Johannes Urzidil, There Goes Kafka, *translated by Harold A. Basilius, 1968, by permission of Wayne State University Press.*

21

individual characteristics become fused into a totality of beauty that does not lend itself to analysis.

The German literary artists and writers of Prague had simultaneous access to at least four ethnic sources, viz., to the Germans to whom they were related by culture and language, to the Czechs who surrounded them in everyday life, to the Jews who historically served as a basic and pervasive factor of the city, and finally to the Austrians, among whom they were born and raised and with whom they shared a common destiny, regardless of whether they viewed this destiny positively or critically. Each of these sources, in turn, derived their respective dynamics from two spheres, namely, the staid, aboriginal inhabitants of the city of Prague and the centripetal surge of the Bohemians. The Bohemians comprised, in part, recent settlers in Prague, and in part also Sudeten-Germans who were attracted to the German University in Prague. Also included were a nucleus of Czech peasants and their descendants gravitating to the provincial, later the state, capital, as well as landed Czech and German Jews from the country who as lesser landowners or lessees represented a unique group. Finally, there was the native Bohemian Austrian nobility, some of them original Czech aristocrats, some of them Austro-Germans, but all of them characterized by a monarchical Austrian orientation. These nobles had palaces in the city as well as imposing country estates throughout Bohemia. Their origins reached far back in time, in some cases as far back as the thirteenth century and the Přemyslide kings. Thus, even the Habsburgers seemed to some of these Czech nobles like relatively recent arrivals. All of the foregoing factors became cumulative, and a literary artist was confronted with this accumulation. As a consequence he removed quickly from a locally circumscribed atmosphere to a larger and more fundamental one.

For the German writers of Prague, the occasionally friendly, but mostly politically turbulent and brawling symbiosis and interaction, not entirely free of anti-Semitic coloration on the part of the Czechs, this glowing of the alchemistic melting pot of Prague, constituted the prime cause of an unrestricted literary spirit which rapidly created its own literary expression on all levels and for which the movement known at that time as expressionism provided a powerful means of release. For Prague by means of its rich national, social, and religious facets did in fact present them with the spiritual potential of a universal megalopolis, much more brilliant than many a larger European metropolis.

An independent German-language literature had indeed formerly existed in Prague and we can clearly discern its roots by pursuing Goethe's relation to Bohemia and the subsequent efforts of the

"Forty-eighters" as well as those of the slightly younger literary artists of the "liberal era," who in the persons of Friedrich Adler and Hugo Salus even extended over into my own youthful development. Rilke also owed a debt to that "liberal era," though he was the leader of the escape of Prague German writers into the European theater of thought, feeling and activity. The epoch whose productions subsequently achieved through Kafka and Werfel a universal acceptance under the decisive influence of Max Brod dates back to Rilke. That sort of thing never before resulted from Prague though during the entire nineteenth century German was so extensively spoken there that the Golden Capital of the Czechs with its hundred towers was regarded superficially by the uninformed almost as a German city, a misinterpretation which was later to have bitter consequences.

Rilke had experienced the Czech milieu at second remove through the people themselves. "The folkish Czech melody" *("Böhmisches Volkes Weise")* resounded in his ears and may have provided him with many a word-form or the turn of a sentence. That is a destiny from which no man can or should exclude himself, for it represents a personal enrichment. But in time Rilke turned away from Prague. He had lived all too briefly with the people and the events of the city and its country, had shared their woes and good fortunes all too little. But all this would not apply to writers such as Paul Leppin, or Franz Werfel, or Paul Kornfeld, or Max Brod, or Felix Weltsch, the philosopher, or the religiously sophisticated Hugo Bergmann, or Willy Haas, the critical mentor, or Erwin Egon Kisch, the "crazy reporter *(rasender Reporter)."* Obviously all this would apply least of all to Franz Kafka, in whom Prague abode just as Zürich did in Keller or Concord in Thoreau. All the inhabitants of Prague I have mentioned lived with the city, owed her their best, became witnesses of the growing political vehemence of the Czechs, of the gradually declining vitality of the Habsburg monarchy, but also and at the same time in the area of German literature, of which they were spiritual co-inhabitants, they witnessed the liberation of the powers of literary expression from the residues of the Baumbach era of liberal doggerel. In the midst of this revolutionary process they could be more supernational precisely in Prague than anywhere else in the German countries.

By virtue of language as well as atmosphere they had direct access to the great Russians. I, for example, read Tolstoy and Dostoevsky not only in German translation but also in Czech. Hence, I could comprehend these authors not only by virtue of reason but also from common heartfelt linguistic relationships. Modern Czech painting, radically and heroically avant-garde, opened up broad vistas toward France. The enormous natural musicality of the Czechs surrounded us, and the best evidences of the Wagnerism cultivated in Prague but now already in decline were being surpassed by the works of a new musical epoch under the leadership of the Austrian Alexander von Zemlinsky, the teacher and brother-in-law of Schönberg. Of course, we neither could nor wanted to withdraw from the influences of Gerhard Hauptmann and Frank Wedekind in the drama, or from those of Stefan George and Hugo von Hofmannsthal in lyric poetry, and yet the German literary part of Prague remained an autochthonous, indeed, a spiritually autarchic world, which by way of example no longer really understood and indeed completely rejected a Karl Kraus, writing from Vienna though he was a native of Central Bohemia.

However, the sentimental magic of Prague, which once caused the verses of Adler and Salus to resound with Gothic and Baroque wizardry, could no longer provide relief for the artistic emotions of the German expressionists living there. They were attracted instead by the close realistic aspects of life, the continuous flux, wherein the godhead resides (Goethe), the social, the humane and world-friendly (Werfel), the totally European, toward which precisely this city of never-ending aggressive antitheses provoked challenges by the hour. This being the case, the German writers of Prague were a much more supranational lot than the Czechs, bound by nationalist sentiments, or the Sudeten-Germans out in the country. [I edited a literary journal for a while and called it simply *Man (Der Mensch)*. It was intended to be a general universal platform for German and Czech writers. It lasted only a short year, for "what achievements by man could have lasting value?" (Goethe).]

Prague was a city of raconteurs, of magical realists, of the narrator with a precise imagination (Goethe: *exakte Phantasie*). It is true that Werfel was a widely heard lyrical herald, and the ethically reputable Rudolf Fuchs, a pure and profound lyricist. It is equally true that Paul Kornfeld was one of the protagonists of the German expressionistic drama. But the most far-reaching and decisive literary achievements were attained in the German prose of Prague. This prose penetrated most effectively far out into the world, for it was completely free of any restricting provincialism and commanded the broadest vistas, a prose in which before long those writers also participated who had been attracted to the magnetic field of Prague from the outside, novelists such as Ernst Weiss, Hermann Ungar, and Ludwig Winder (all three, Moravians), Oskar Baum or Melchior Vischer (both from Inner Bohemia). In the Prague of that day they became exponents of the demands for general spiritual freedom of man and of the world.

Today as I recall that Prague it seems to me in essence a Kafkaesque city. This may seem self-evident and almost trivial nowadays but I, and not only I, felt that way already when Kafka was still there among us in Prague. Although Prague is reflected in Kafka's work at best only in occasional paraphrase, it nonetheless pervades all of his writing just as salt pervades the water in that Buddhist parable. Though the salt as such is not visible, the water tastes thoroughly salty. In precisely the same way one can document the immanence of Prague in every character, every situation, and every description from Kafka's pen. A single example: Following the publication of "The Metamorphosis," Kafka remarked to my father-in-law Professor Karl Thieberger during a casual meeting on the street: "What do you have to say about the dreadful things happening in our house?" This might seem funny to anyone not knowing Kafka. It was irony, to be sure, as most everything was to Kafka, but not only irony. It was also serious realism.

Czech literary artists and writers, most of them still deeply immersed in their national struggle for survival, could not, however, surrender themselves so easily to that kind of fundamentalism, though indications of it were appearing in the writings of the brothers Josef and Karel Čapek and in the works of a number of plastic artists and musicians striving for universal recognition, in short, in works whose form was calculated to achieve most quickly and directly an artistic world-status though retaining the national stigma. For this reason the personal relations of the German literary artists and writers of Prague to Czech painters and musicians was more viable than their relations to Czech writers. The grotesque nature of the language barrier also contributed to this situation. Not all German literary folk in Prague had a good command of the Czech language (except for several Jews among them), and only a few of the Czech authors could or wanted to speak German.

At the time of Kafka's major productivity, Prague was most typically Prague and also most typically Kafkaesque. The actual essence of that city can be grasped and defined more completely through Kafka than any other writer, and certainly through him rather than any Czech literary work, though one such latter would seem especially predestined to portray the city. This fact is probably one of the involuntary reasons why some Czech literati have repeatedly tried to represent Kafka as being a kind of Czech in disguise and thus to extricate him somewhat from German literature by sleight of hand. Among other things, the American practice of determining nationality according to the country of one's birth has been, incidentally, useful in furthering efforts to classify Kafka as a "Czech writer." This is patently absurd, for an author belongs to the spiritual representation of the language in which he thinks and writes. [When Kafka once wrote to his Czech girl-friend Milena Jesenská: "German is my mother-tongue and hence natural to me though Czech is much dearer to my heart"—one must keep in mind that this utterance is not a "literary" statement but one addressed to and fashioned for his Czech sweetheart. Czech doubtless had a "hearty" sound also for Rilke as it does for everyone who knows this language in native terms and who perhaps grew up in a Czech environment (just as Kafka, Rilke, Brod, as well as the author of this book did) or knew how to speak the language.]

Our Prague German, frequently enough maligned and certainly not lacking in accent though free of all dialect, was able to preserve itself pure and unadulterated on that isolated language island of Prague since the middle ages precisely because it was not exposed to the whittling and dialectal affects of the German used in the provinces and in the country. This was a unique blessing for literature, for we Prague Germans wrote and continue to write in the language in which we live and talk day-in and day-out. Yet this was also true of Karl Egon Ebert or of Rainer Maria Rilke or of Egon Erwin Kisch. There was never a chasm between the literary and the common language for the Prague Germans. No inner necessity to shift, regardless of how unconscious it might be, was ever necessary. This complete coincidence of daily speech with that of literature is probably the great and powerful secret of the Prague German writers with respect to form and effect. It was especially true of Kafka. Anyone hearing him speak also heard him in every line he wrote down to the subtlest nuance. This is the secret of inner identity which we Prague Germans cherished and preserved as long as possible and which is now, of course, disappearing with the last of us.

Michel Carrouges

The Struggle Against the Father

In 1920, a year after Kafka had written the "Letter to His Father," the young Gustav Janouch, who had greatly admired Franz Kafka even before making his acquaintance, set down a firsthand account of the following incident, which he had witnessed one evening in Prague:

> My first walk with Franz Kafka ended in the following way:
> Our circuit of the [Altstädter] Ring had brought us back to the Kinsky Palace, when from out of the warehouse, with the business sign HERMANN KAFKA, emerged a tall, broad man in a dark overcoat and a shining hat. He remained standing about five steps away from us and waited.
> As we came three paces nearer, the man said, very loudly:
> "Franz. Go home. The air is damp."
> Kafka said, in a strangely gentle voice:
> "My father. He is anxious about me. Love often wears the face of violence. Come and see me."
> I bowed. Franz Kafka departed, without shaking hands.[1]

Some time later, Janouch saw Kafka, who had just returned from a visit to the country, and said to him:

> "So now we are at home again."
> Kafka smiled sadly.

[1] *Conversations with Kafka*: Gustav Janouch's record of his and Kafka's conversations, set down at the time of their relationship (1920-1923), p. 31.

Reprinted by permission from Michel Carrouges, Kafka versus Kafka, *translated by Emmett Parker, 1958, by the University of Alabama Press, University, Alabama.*

"At home? I live with my parents. That is all. It is true I have a small room of my own, but that is not a home, only a place of refuge, where I can hide my inner turmoil, only in order to fall all the more into its clutches."[2]

At that time, Franz, who was thirty-seven and a bachelor, was already suffering from tuberculosis, which explains his living at home and his father's urgent solicitude; but the tyranny inherent in this situation was none the less evident.

The situation, moreover, was very complicated, for Kafka's attitude was one neither of total rebellion nor of complete submission. Franz considered his father a superior type of man whom he envied and whom he found objectionable at the same time. He did not wish to be the kind of man his father was, and he could not have been.

In a letter written to F. B. in 1916 he strongly underlined the extreme ambivalence of his feelings:

However, I am descended from my parents, am linked to them and my sisters by blood, am sensible of it neither in my everyday affairs nor, as a result of their inevitable familiarity to me, in my special concerns, but at bottom have more respect for it than I realize.[3]

To which he immediately added:

Sometimes this bond of blood too is the target of my hatred; the sight of the double bed at home, the used sheets, the nightshirts carefully laid out, can exasperate me to the point of nausea, can turn me inside out . . . .[4]

All that Kafka says about his love for his mother, his sisters, and even for his father can be found in the letter to his father. Never does Franz address Hermann in a tone of hatred, scorn, or even cold indifference. Rarely have such grave reproaches been expressed with such delicacy, such gentleness, and with such a desire not to offend someone who himself never ceased to offend. The son so scrupulously analyzes his relations with his father that he stresses every possibility of interpretation that might justify his parent. Kafka felt everything deeply, yet he surmounted it all. The letter begins:

[2] *Ibid.*, p. 40.
[3] Franz Kafka, *Diaries: 1914-23*, p. 167.
[4] *Ibid.*

Dear Father:
You asked me recently why I maintain that I am afraid of you. As usual, I was unable to think of any answer to your question, partly for the very reason that I am afraid of you, and partly because an explanation of the grounds for this fear would mean going into far more details than I could even approximately keep in mind while talking.[5]

This opening suffices to set the tone of the whole letter written in 1919. Sometimes, when one misreads Kafka's novels, one finds them systematically long and interminable, indeed boring, because one judges things summarily. What one had thought to be simple, rapid, and clear, Kafka pitilessly reveals (primarily for himself, but for us also), as complex, broad in scope, and obscure. Thereby he teaches us to see what we did not previously know how to see. In the letter to his father, however, as on every occasion when he deems it well to do so—at the beginning of his novels, for example—he goes directly to the heart of the burning question.

How to understand that fear of his father? That is what he seeks to explain interminably, for the subject is indeed inexhaustible. The basis for that fear was his father's "intellectual domination,"[6] a term oppressive in its meaning and, at the same time, filled with unspeakable irony:

You had worked your way up so far alone, by your own energies, and as a result you had unbounded confidence in your opinion. . . . From your armchair you ruled the world. Your opinion was correct, every other was mad, wild, *meshugge*, not normal.[7]

Kafka saw in his father the very "ideal" of the paterfamilias, the man who is capable of establishing a household, of governing his wife and children, of having a profession that enables him to feed his family and to make his way in society. In order to accomplish all this, he says:

What is essential . . . is what I have recognized in you, and indeed everything rolled into one, good and bad, as it is organically combined in you, that is to say, strength, and scorn of the other, health and a certain immoderation, eloquence and inadequacy, self-confidence and dissatisfaction with everyone else, a superior

[5] Franz Kafka, *Dearest Father*, p. 5.
[6] *Ibid.*, p. 145.
[7] *Ibid.*

attitude to the world and tyranny, knowledge of human nature and mistrust of most people, then also good qualities without any drawback, such as industry, endurance, presence of mind, and fearlessness.[8]

Kafka adds, however: "Of all this I had by comparison almost nothing or only very little. . . ."[9]

Some might be inclined to conclude from the son's apology, ironic as it is, that his father was an extraordinary man, although, as Max Brod points out, Franz exaggerated his father's qualities. While this is quite evident, Kafka did not exaggerate the antinomy that existed between him and his father, if one tends to see their relationship in terms of the opposition between the man of affairs and the intellectual.

To begin let us turn back to Kafka's childhood memories. It is difficult to choose among the thousand telling details of the father's behavior at table, his methods of punishment, or his outbursts of anger at the store; they could be cited endlessly. It is perhaps of more importance to stress the father's imprecatory side, his long series of not so much pedagogical as Jupterian apostrophes:

> Because in accordance with your strong appetite and your particular habit you ate everything fast, hot and in big mouthfuls, the child had to hurry, there was a somber silence at the table, interrupted by admonitions: "Eat first, talk afterwards." . . . Bones mustn't be cracked with the teeth, but you could. Vinegar must not be sipped noisily, but you could.[10]

> It was only necessary to be happy about something or other, to be filled with the thought of it, to come home and speak of it, and the answer was an ironical sigh, a shaking of the head, a tapping of the table with one finger: "Is that all you're worked up about?" . . . or "What can you buy yourself with that?" or "What a song and dance about nothing!"[11]

> How terrible for me was, for instance, that "I'll tear you apart like a fish," in spite of knowing, of course, that there was nothing worse to follow (admittedly, as a little child I didn't know that), but it was almost exactly in accord with my notions of your power and I saw you as being capable of doing this too.[12]

[8]*Ibid.,* pp. 192-193.
[9]*Ibid.*
[10]*Ibid.*, p. 148.
[11]*Ibid.*, p. 146.
[12]*Ibid.*, p. 152.

What was also maddening were those rebukes when one was treated as a third person, in other words accounted not worthy even to be spoken to angrily: that is to say, when you would speak in form to Mother but in fact to me, sitting there at the same time. For instance: "Of course, that's too much to expect of our worthy son" and the like.[13]

Each incident, if one speaks only of isolated cases, amounted to no more than a drop of water, but as they accumulated, day after day, throughout the course of the years, they could no longer be considered as isolated. The single drops of water had become an ocean of bitterness; finally they became a tidal wave and catastrophe struck:

The impossibility of getting on calmly together had one more result, actually a very natural one: *I lost the capacity to talk* [my italics]. I dare say I would never have been a very eloquent person in any case, but I would, after all, have had the usual fluency of human language at my command. But at a very early stage you forbade me to talk. Your threat: "Not a word of contradiction!" and the raised hand that accompanied it have gone with me ever since. What I got from you—and you are, as soon as it is a matter of your own affairs, an excellent talker—was a hesitant, stammering mode of speech, and even that was still too much for you, and finally I kept silent, at first perhaps from defiance, and then because I couldn't either think or speak in your presence. And because you were the person who really brought me up, this has had its repercussions throughout my life.[14]

Kafka wrote, in fact, as early as 1913, in a projected letter to Felicia B.'s father:

. . . I live in my family, among the best and most lovable people, more strange than a stranger. I have not spoken an average of twenty words a day to my mother these last years, hardly ever said more than a hello to my father. I do not speak at all to my married sisters and my brothers-in-law, and not because I have anything against them. The reason for it is simply this, that I have not the slightest thing to talk to them about. *Everything that is not literature bores me and I hate it* . . . [my italics].[15]

This last statement may seem surprising: some will insist that it

[13] *Ibid.*, p. 153.
[14] *Ibid.*, pp. 150-151.
[15] Franz Kafka, *Diaries: 1910-13*, pp. 299-300.

reflects the egotism of the man of letters, the stale detachment of the intellectual, the narcissism of the writer, and other phrases of the same stamp that only serve to avoid confronting the real issues. In fact, there is a tragic and intimate link between this remark in the letter to Felicia's father and the brutally overwhelming statement revealing the catastrophe that had occurred in Kafka's childhood world: "I lost the capacity to talk." Aphasia, occurring mainly in the mind and in a relative sense of the word, but aphasia nonetheless. For dialogue is a vital necessity, and an upbringing without dialogue between parent and child can only be monstrous. Kafka was aware of this: between the father and the son the barrier of silence grew higher, expanded indefinitely, and finally formed truly a "Great Wall of China." In an ultimate assault Franz tried one day to open a breach in the wall of silence, but only by means of a letter, a letter he could not even mail or give to his father; he could only give it to his mother, and she decided that it was impossible to deliver it to its intended recipient. As in Kafka's writings, the message can only come too late, after death. It is we, strangers, who receive Kafka's message, which was not destined for us. Out of the silence between father and son, like a poisoned spring, flow other rivers of silence between Franz and his family, between Franz and the people he met, even between him and the women he tried to love, because the distance between Kafka's inner self and the exterior world had become too great.

There is another side to this silence, however. It is not the empty silence of the yogi, but the overflowing silence of suppressed words, of sensitivity turned inward, of thoughts returning endlessly to their source.

What in fact is an intimate diary such as Kafka's if not the beach where one finds the flotsam and jetsam of suffering and the treasures that the mainstream of life has rejected? What is literature, when it aims at something more than facile amusement or commercialism, if not the inverse reflection of what life has produced and rejected? It is for that very reason that the work of art produces a catharsis, that is to say, liberates, because it surrenders the body to phantoms that haunt the mind and projects these phantoms into the exterior world. . . .

If Kafka reveals to us today many secrets of the human consciousness, it is because he was capable of exorcising from his being immemorial prohibitions imposed by an inner sense of guilt. If he was capable of doing so, it was because he was forced in that direction by an illegitimate, external prohibition that hindered him from giving ordinary expression to his inner thoughts. But Hermann Kafka could not have foreseen this, no more than the Sultan could have imagined that in barring the route to the Indies, he "forced" Columbus to discover the New World.

Franz wrote to his father:

> ... You have a dislike in advance of every one of my activities and particularly of the nature of my interest. ...[16]
>
> This applied to thoughts as well as to people. It was enough that I should take a little interest in a person—which in any case did not happen often, as a result of my nature—for you, without any consideration for my feelings or respect for my judgment to butt in with abuse, defamation, and denigration. Innocent, childlike people, such as, for instance, the Yiddish actor Löwy, had to pay for that. Without knowing him you compared him, in a dreadful way that I have now forgotten, to vermin and as was so often the case with people I was fond of you were automatically ready with the proverb of the dog and its fleas.*[17]

Nor was such behavior on his father's part limited to Kafka's young childhood or merely to friends. When Franz alluded to one of his proposed marriages, his father crushed him with sarcasm:

> What you said to me was more or less as follows: "She probably put on some specially chosen blouse, the thing these Prague Jewesses are good at, and straightway, of course, you made up your mind to marry her. And, what's more, as fast as possible ..." ... You have, I suppose, scarcely ever humiliated me more deeply with words and have never more clearly shown me your contempt. ... Of my attempts to escape in other directions you knew nothing ... and had to try and guess at them, and your guess was in keeping with your total judgment of me, a guess at the most abominable, crude, and ridiculous thing possible.[18]

Kafka's heart was devastated. But this does not tell the whole story, for at the same time all that the heart gives life to was similarly devastated: all sense of life, all human relationships. Kafka's admirable intelligence could no longer reflect anything but an almost desperate, nocturnal world of ruins peopled by phantoms.

[16] Kafka, *Dearest Father*, p. 175.
[17] *Ibid.*, pp. 146-147.
[18] *Ibid.*, pp. 187-188.

Wer sich mit Hunden niederlegt, steht mit Flöhen auf. Who lies down with dogs gets up with fleas [trans. note].

Yet, this heart was ceaselessly reborn intact, thirsting for love, incapable of blindness or hatred, never forgetting that there were hours in that hell that were at once painful and exquisite.

> Fortunately there were, I admit, exceptions to all these things mostly when you suffered in silence, and affection and kindliness by their own strength overcame all obstacles, and moved me immediately. Admittedly this was rare, but it was wonderful. For instance, when in earlier times, in hot summers, when you were tired after lunch, I saw you having a nap at the office, your elbow on the desk; or when you joined us in the country, in the summer holidays, on Sundays, worn out from work at the office; or the time when Mother was gravely ill and you stood holding on to the bookcase, shaking with sobs; or when, during my last illness, you came tiptoeing to Ottla's* room to see me, stopping in the doorway, craning your neck to see me, and out of consideration for me only waved your hand to me. At such times one would lie back and weep for happiness, and one weeps again now, writing it down. You have a particularly beautiful, very rare way of quietly, contentedly, approvingly smiling. . . .[19]

Wondrous moments that Kafka did not forget; but neither did he fail to realize that they had had, by contrast, only one other result: to render his suffering more vivid, to increase his "sense of guilt" and to make the world for him "still more incomprehensible."[20]

> . . . In all my thinking I was, after all, under the heavy pressure of your personality, even in that part of it—and particularly in that—which was not in accord with yours. All these thoughts, seemingly independent of yours, were from the beginning loaded with the burden of your harsh and dogmatic judgments . . . .[21]

Such is the balance sheet of the perverse upbringing that Franz Kafka was subjected to. It may even be called a model upbringing in reverse. Franz summed up in a word its result when he concluded his long letter: "Not even your mistrust of yours, after all, is as great as my self-mistrust, which you inculcated in me."[22] It is from this point in

---

[19] *Ibid.*, p. 155.
[20] *Ibid.*
[21] *Ibid.*, p. 145.
[22] *Ibid.*, p. 196.

*One of Franz's sisters.

the relationship with his father that the black sun* shines tragically, obstinately, on all aspects of Kafka's life:

> Marrying is barred to me through the fact that it is precisely and peculiarly your most intimate domain.[23]

> ... Since nothing was in my very own, undoubted, sole possession, determined unequivocally only by me—in sober truth a disinherited son—naturally even the thing nearest at hand, my own body, became insecure.[24]

> ... I was given the liberty to choose my career. But was I still at all capable of really making use of such liberty? Had I still my confidence in my own capacity to achieve a real career?[25] I could not but side with the staff [at his father's store].[26] I found equally little means of escape from you in Judaism.[27]

> My writing was all about you; all I did there, after all, was to bemoan what I could not bemoan upon your breast.[28]

On every side, Kafka came up against the prodigious specter of his father, a dark Proteus blocking all exits. In the face of such a presence, there was no other means of revolt and salvation except flight. That is the way out that Kafka finally took when he left for Berlin with Dora Dymant in 1923. By then it was too late.

Oedipus complex? No doubt. But, let us please avoid reducing the numberless varied experiences of Oedipus' tragedy to mechanical variants of an explanatory gimmick that is never any more than the beginning of an explanation. For the further one goes the more one sees that one is entering into a labyrinth of explanations. The more light is shed into the wings offstage, the more wings one discovers, deeper, ever more numerous, more mysterious still than one had begun to suspect. The true power of psychoanalysis is that it explains the myth a good

[23] *Ibid.*, p. 191.
[24] *Ibid.*, p. 178.
[25] *Ibid.*, p. 179.
[26] *Ibid.*, p. 162.
[27] *Ibid.*, p. 171.
[28] *Ibid.*, p. 177.

*An allusion to the "black sun of Melancholy" from Gérard de Nerval's *El Desdichado*—". . . et mon luth constellé/Porte le *soleil noir* de la *Mélancholie*"—which in turn was inspired by Albrecht Dürer's engraving *Melancholia* in which strong rays of sunlight beat down upon the contemplative allegorical figure of Melancholy [trans. note].

deal less by way of the complex than the complex by way of the myth; the very nature of myth is to be inexhaustible and fathomless.

This too Kafka was aware of. He had Freud in mind when he wrote "The Judgment," but he objected to the claims of psychoanalysts of having arrived at definitive explanations. Kafka knew how to probe ever deeper and further. "The revolt of the son against the father," he said one day to Janouch, "is one of the primeval themes of literature. . . ." It is a tragedy, or rather a comedy, Franz added with bitter irony, and in support he cited Synge's play *The Playboy of the Western World*, in which a rebellious son brags of having bludgeoned his father, but who then finds himself embarrassed and reduced to an untenable situation by the reappearance of the "old man." "I see you are very skeptical," exclaimed Janouch. ". . . This struggle is usually only shadow boxing," Franz replied. "Age is the future of youth, which sooner or later it must reach. So why struggle? To become old sooner? For a quicker departure?"[29] By which we may understand: The struggle is real enough, but its result is ephemeral, therefore without real substance. Why struggle, since death in any case comes to end everything? There all human combat finally fails. But the very nature of youth and of adulthood is precisely to make of death an "abstraction," to struggle and to live as though death did not exist.

This idea expressed to Janouch sums up the defeat of Franz, crushed by the destructive tyranny of his father, and devoted, like the son in "The Judgment," to making of his existence nothing more than a multiform and prolonged suicide, but a suicide all the same.

The unbreathable atmosphere of Kafka's tales is not, then, a gratuitous invention of his imagination; his art flows out of the conflict with his father, it manifests that conflict and re-creates it all over again. In the letter to his father he wrote:

> You struck nearer home with your dislike of my writing and all that, unknown to you, was connected with it. Here I had, in fact, got some distance away from you by my own efforts, even if it was slightly reminiscent of the worm that, as a foot tramples on the tail end of it, breaks loose with its top end and drags itself aside. To a certain extent I was in safety; there was a chance to breathe freely.[30]

Art here reflects the positive phase of the force of reaction. The attempt to escape beyond the paternal sphere appears then as a valid and even successful attempt. But this is only the initial phase, for there is the inevitable shock of the counter-reaction:

[29] *Conversations with Kafka*, pp. 41-42.
[30] Kafka, *Dearest Father*, p. 176.

My vanity and my ambition did suffer, it is true, under your soon proverbial way of hailing the arrival of my books: "Put it on my bedside table!" (as it happened, you were usually playing cards when a book came). . . .[31]

As in every dialogue, communication between father and son could have taken two paths: the short path of the spoken word or the long path of the written word. Between Hermann and Franz the short path was cut off. The long path seems to have been cut off as well, since father and son lived nearly always with one another and since Franz tried only once, at the age of thirty-six, to write that finally free and open letter, which is all the more interminable for having been interminably postponed. But in the final analysis it was a message that could not be delivered to its intended recipient, for in actuality Franz dared only give it to his mother, and she in turn did not dare to transmit it to her husband. As in *The Castle*, women have the power of intercession, but it is a power so limited as to be practically useless.

Thus there remained for Franz only one desperate possibility of hope: to take a path parallel to the long path by substituting for the outright letter, addressed to his father designated by name, a cryptographic message woven into symbolic fictions charged with allusions and addressed as though to someone offstage. Was this not the logical extension of the manner in which the father spoke of his son in the third person, addressing the mother in the son's presence? But this path too had already been tried and Franz knew the result. In 1913 and 1916 he had published "The Judgment" and "The Metamorphosis," which seem to us as atrociously clear as they did to him, but the long path and veiled language could not succeed any better than other methods in reestablishing communication between father and son, for every attempt ended at the closed gate to the short path, crushed by that abrupt exclamation: "Put it on my bedside table!"

Needless to say, in spite of Franz's humble remark, all of this infinitely surpasses the minor matter of a wound to his literary vanity, for Hermann's taste was truly devoid of importance. What Franz resented so frightfully was that not even affected or willful disdain with regard to his most profound drama.

Suffering is all the more keen when there is no way out, no recourse. Far from being alone in his attitude, the father could assert that the whole family circle joined him in it. One Sunday when the family was gathered at Kafka's grandparents' home, enjoying an

[31] *Ibid.*, pp. 176-177.

afternoon snack, Franz noted on a scrap of paper, not without some spirit of provocation, several impressions for a future novel:

> An uncle who liked to make fun of people finally took the page that I was holding only weakly, looked at it briefly, handed it back to me, even without laughing, and only said to the others who were following him with their eyes, "The usual stuff," to me he said nothing.[32]

Of course, Hermann might well have added, "My dear son can only write grotesque and absurd things without the slightest relation to the solidly real and affectionate life that we all lead." But how can we reproach Hermann when even today writers who have at their fingertips all the evidence still affirm seriously that all of Kafka's writings are unreal, phantasmagoric, and barren of significance.

Franz, however, categorically stated his case in that same letter to his father:

> My writing was all about you; all I did there, after all, was to bemoan what I could not bemoan upon your breast. It was an intentionally long-drawn-out leave-taking from you, only although it was brought about by force on your part, it did not take its course in the direction determined by me.[33]

If Kafka's short stories and novels are reread in the light of this perspective, one will see that apart from many other significant aspects, they conceal within them first of all a significant familial and more especially, a paternal orientation that is central to them. In certain of these tales, it is baldly apparent, notably in "The Judgment." The same can be said for the story of Odradek, which bears the title "The Cares of a Family Man."*

The meaning of "The Metamorphosis" must also be reconsidered in this light. Is it not from one end to the other the story of a young man whose mysterious illness results in a change in him that renders him incapable of a normal life and unrecognizable to his own loved ones? The "bizarre" aspect of Gregor Samsa's case is clarified by converging rays of light: in addition to foreshadowing Kafka's tuberculosis, it symbolizes the monstrous familial peculiarity of Kafka's genius.

---

[32] Kafka, *Diaries: 1910-13,* p. 44.
[33] Kafka, *Dearest Father,* p. 177.

The Penal Colony (New York: Schocken, 1961), pp. 160-161.

W. H. Auden

The I Without a Self

> The joys of this life are not its own, but our
> dread of ascending to a higher life: the tor-
> ments of this life are not its own, but our self-
> torment because of that dread. —Franz Kafka

Remarkable as *The Trial* and *The Castle* are, Kafka's finest work, I
think, is to be found in the volume *The Great Wall of China*, all of it
written during the last six years of his life. The world it portrays is still
the world of his earlier books and one cannot call it euphoric, but the
tone is lighter. The sense of appalling anguish and despair which make
stories like "The Penal Colony" [sic] almost unbearable, has gone.
Existence may be as difficult and frustrating as ever, but the characters
are more humorously resigned to it.

Of a typical story one might say that it takes the formula of the
heroic Quest and turns it upside down. In the traditional Quest, the
goal—a Princess, the Fountain of Life, etc.—is known to the hero before
he starts. This goal is far distant and he usually does not know in
advance the way thither nor the dangers which beset it, but there are
other beings who know both and give him accurate directions and
warnings. Moreover the goal is publicly recognizable as desirable.
Everybody would like to achieve it, but it can only be reached by the
Predestined Hero. When three brothers attempt the Quest in turn, the
first two are found wanting and fail because of their arrogance and
self-conceit, while the youngest succeeds, thanks to his humility and

Reprinted from W. H. Auden, The Dyer's Hand *(1962), by permission
of Random House and Faber and Faber.*

kindness of heart. But the youngest, like his two elders, is always perfectly confident that he will succeed.

In a typical Kafka story, on the other hand, the goal is peculiar to the hero himself: he has no competitors. Some beings whom he encounters try to help him, more are obstructive, most are indifferent, and none has the faintest notion of the way. As one of the aphorisms puts it: "There is a goal but no way; what we call the way is mere wavering." Far from being confident of success, the Kafka hero is convinced from the start that he is doomed to fail, as he is also doomed, being who he is, to make prodigious and unending efforts to reach it. Indeed, the mere desire to reach the goal is itself a proof, not that he is one of the Elect, but that he is under a special curse.

> Perhaps there is only one cardinal sin: impatience. Because of impatience we were driven out of Paradise, because of impatience we cannot return.

> Theoretically, there exists a perfect possibility of happiness: to believe in the indestructible element in oneself and not strive after it.

In all previous versions of the Quest, the hero knows what he ought to do and his one problem is "Can I do it?" Odysseus knows he must not listen to the song of the sirens, a knight in quest of the Sangreal knows he must remain chaste, a detective knows he must distinguish between truth and falsehood. But for K the problem is "What ought I to do?" He is neither tempted, confronted with a choice between good and evil, nor carefree, content with the sheer exhilaration of motion. He is certain that it matters enormously what he does *now*, without knowing at all what that ought to be. If he *guesses* wrong, he must not only suffer the same consequences as if he had *chosen* wrong, but also feel the same responsibility. If the instructions and advice he receives seem to him absurd or contradictory, he cannot interpret this as evidence of malice or guilt in others; it may well be proof of his own.

The traditional Quest Hero has *arete*, either manifest, like Odysseus, or concealed, like the fairy tale hero; in the first case, successful achievement of the Quest adds to his glory, in the second it reveals that the apparent nobody is a glorious hero: to become a hero, in the traditional sense, means acquiring the right, thanks to one's exceptional gifts and deeds, to say *I*. But K is an *I* from the start, and in this fact alone, that he exists, irrespective of any gifts or deeds, lies his guilt.

If the K of *The Trial* were innocent, he would cease to be K and become nameless like the fawn in the wood in *Through the Looking-*

Glass. In *The Castle*, K, the letter, wants to become a word, *land-surveyor*, that is to say, to acquire a self like everybody else but this is precisely what he is not allowed to acquire.

The world of the traditional quest may be dangerous, but it is open: the hero can set off in any direction he fancies. But the Kafka world is closed; though it is almost devoid of sensory properties, it is an intensely physical world. The objects and faces in it may be vague, but the reader feels himself hemmed in by their suffocating presence: in no other imaginary world, I think, is everything so *heavy*. To take a single step exhausts the strength. The hero feels himself to be a prisoner and tries to escape but perhaps imprisonment is the proper state for which he was created, and freedom would destroy him.

> The more horse you yoke, the quicker everything will go—not the rending of the block from its foundation, which is impossible, but the snapping of the traces and with that the gay and empty journey.

The narrator hero of "The Burrow," for example, is a beast of unspecified genus, but, presumably, some sort of badger-like animal, except that he is carnivorous. He lives by himself without a mate and never encounters any other member of his own species. He also lives in a perpetual state of fear lest he be pursued and attacked by other animals—"My enemies are countless," he says—but we never learn what they may be like and we never actually encounter one. His preoccupation is with the burrow which has been his lifework. Perhaps, when he first began excavating this, the idea of a burrow-fortress was more playful than serious, but the bigger and better the burrow becomes, the more he is tormented by the question: "Is it possible to construct the absolutely impregnable burrow?" This is a torment because he can never be certain that there is not some further precaution of which he has not thought. Also the burrow he has spent his life constructing has become a precious thing which he must defend as much as he would defend himself.

> One of my favorite plans was to isolate the Castle Keep from its surroundings, that is to say to restrict the thickness of the walls to about my own height, and leave a free space of about the same width all around the Castle Keep . . . I had always pictured this free space, and not without reason, as the loveliest imaginable haunt. What a joy to lie pressed against the rounded outer wall, pull oneself up, let oneself slide down again, miss one's footing and find oneself on firm earth, and play all these games literally upon the

Castle Keep and not inside it; to avoid the Castle Keep, to rest one's eyes from it whenever one wanted, to postpone the joy of seeing it until later and yet not have to do without it, but literally hold it safe between one's claws. . . .

He begins to wonder if, in order to defend it, it would not be better to hide in the bushes outside near its hidden entrance and keep watch. He considers the possibility of enlisting the help of a confederate to share the task of watching, but decides against it.

. . . would he not demand some counter-service from me; would he not at least want to see the burrow? That in itself, to let anyone freely into my burrow, would be exquisitely painful to me. I built it for myself, not for visitors, and I think I would refuse to admit him . . . I simply could not admit him, for either I must let him go in first by himself, which is simply unimaginable, or we must both descend at the same time, in which case the advantage I am supposed to derive from him, that of being kept watch over, would be lost. And what trust can I really put in him? . . . It is comparatively easy to trust any one if you are supervising him or at least supervise him; perhaps it is possible to trust some one at a distance; but completely to trust some one outside the burrow when you are inside the burrow, that is, in a different world, that, it seems to me, is impossible.

One morning he is awakened by a faint whistling noise which he cannot identify or locate. It might be merely the wind, but it might be some enemy. From now on, he is in the grip of a hysterical anxiety. Does this strange beast, if it is a beast, know of his existence and, if so, what does it know. The story breaks off without a solution. Edwin Muir has suggested that the story would have ended with the appearance of the invisible enemy to whom the hero would succumb. I am doubtful about this. The whole point of the parable seems to be that the reader is never to know if the narrator's subjective fears have any objective justification.

The more we admire Kafka's writings, the more seriously we must reflect upon his final instructions that they should be destroyed. At first one is tempted to see in this request a fantastic spiritual pride, as if he had said to himself: "To be worthy of me, anything I write must be absolutely perfect. But no piece of writing, however excellent, can be perfect. Therefore, let what I have written be destroyed as unworthy of me." But everything which Dr. Brod and other friends tell us about Kafka as a person makes nonsense of this explanation.

It seems clear that Kafka did not think of himself as an artist in the traditional sense, that is to say, as a being dedicated to a particular function, whose personal existence is accidental to his artistic productions. If there ever was a man of whom it could be said that he "hungered and thirsted after righteousness," it was Kafka. Perhaps he came to regard what he had written as a personal device he had employed in his search for God. "Writing," he once wrote, "is a form of prayer," and no person whose prayers are genuine, desires them to be overheard by a third party. In another passage, he describes his aim in writing thus:

> Somewhat as if one were to hammer together a table with painful and methodical technical efficiency, and simultaneously do nothing at all, and not in such a way that people could say: "Hammering a table together is nothing to him," but rather "Hammering a table together is really hammering a table together to him, but at the same time it is nothing," whereby certainly the hammering would have become still bolder, still surer, still more real, and if you will, still more senseless.

But whatever the reasons, Kafka's reluctance to have his work published should at least make a reader wary of the way in which he himself reads it. Kafka may be one of those writers who are doomed to be read by the wrong public. Those on whom their effect would be most beneficial are repelled and on those whom they most fascinate their effect may be dangerous, even harmful.

I am inclined to believe that one should only read Kafka when one is in a eupeptic state of physical and mental health and, in consequence, tempted to dismiss any scrupulous heart-searching as a morbid fuss. When one is in low spirits, one should probably keep away from him, for, unless introspection is accompanied, as it always was in Kafka, by an equal passion for the good life, it all too easily degenerates into a spineless narcissistic fascination with one's own sin and weakness.

No one who thinks seriously about evil and suffering can avoid entertaining as a possibility the gnostic-manichean notion of the physical world as intrinsically evil, and some of Kafka's sayings come perilously close to accepting it.

> There is only a spiritual world; what we call the physical world is the evil in the spiritual one.

> The physical world is not an illusion, but only its evil which, however, admittedly constitutes our picture of the physical world.

Kafka's own life and his writings as a whole are proof that he was not a gnostic at heart, for the true gnostic can always be recognized by certain characteristics. He regards himself as a member of a spiritual elite and despises all earthly affections and social obligations. Quite often, he also allows himself an anarchic immorality in his sexual life, on the grounds that, since the body is irredeemable, a moral judgment cannot be applied to its actions.

Neither Kafka, as Dr. Brod knew him, nor any of his heroes show a trace of spiritual snobbery nor do they think of the higher life they search for as existing in some other-world sphere: the distinction they draw between *this* world and *the* world does not imply that there are two different worlds, only that our habitual conceptions of reality are not the true conception.

Perhaps, when he wished his writings to be destroyed, Kafka foresaw the nature of too many of his admirers.

Anthony Thorlby

"The Judgment"

[Kafka's first] and apparently harmless meeting [with Felice Bauer] took place on 13 August 1912; but a few days later Kafka recorded the occasion in his diary, concluding his sharp, unflattering description of her appearance with the words: "As I was sitting down I looked at her for the first time more carefully, and when I was seated I had already an unshakeable judgment" [*"hatte ich schon ein unerschütterliches Urteil"*].

How fateful that look was, and how ambiguous that clear judgment! Was it a judgment on her or on himself? Earlier in the diary entry he remarks against himself how alienated he felt "from everything good in its entirety"; and the first masterpiece Kafka wrote, having the title "The Judgment," deals with the fatal consequences—to himself—of a young man's announcement of his engagement in a letter. Two days before Kafka composed this story during a single night of unprecedented inspiration, he had written for the first time to Felice Bauer.

Of this composition, which was to remain Kafka's favorite, partly because of the compelling power with which it had come to him, Kafka nevertheless used the painful image that was to haunt him five years later as a symbolic way of expressing the connection between his writing, his engagement, and his (in his view) self-inflicted tuberculosis: "Then the wound broke open for the first time in one long night." That not only this story, but also probably "Metamorphosis" and above all *The Trial* are intimately connected with Kafka's relationship to Felice Bauer there can be no doubt. Unfortunately, this biographical informa-

From A Student's Guide to Kafka *by Anthony Thorlby, 1972. Reprinted by permission of Heinemann Educational Books, Ltd., London.*

tion does not make the story, perhaps the most mysterious that Kafka ever wrote, any easier to understand.

The transition in this story from a description of commonplace events (a young man writing about his engagement, to a friend living abroad), to an equally matter-of-fact account of very uncommon events (the son's being condemned to death by his father and going out to execute the sentence), is perfectly treated; the texture of the narrative, which is both normal and terrible, is quite seamless. The doddery old father of the first half who rises up at the end to pronounce judgment with the authority and effectiveness of a God-figure still remains at the same time a grotesque old man. His actions and remarks make no more and no less sense at the end than they do at the beginning, but they gradually acquire the power of life and death.

Why does Georg's father have this power over him? About six months after writing the story, Kafka felt prompted to "write down all the relationships which have become clear to me as far as I now remember them"—he was then engaged in reading the proofs—and this particular question of the father's authority he answered as follows:

> ... only because he [Georg] has lost everything except his awareness of the father does the judgment, which closes off his father from him completely, have so strong an effect on him.[1]

The diary entry as a whole stresses the obvious fact about the narrative that at the beginning Georg believes that he has a bond with his father through the figure of his friend, whereas at the end the bond seems to exist only between father and friend to the exclusion of Georg. If we ask again why this should change the father's position of initial weakness into one of such formidable strength, we find that what has really changed is the plausibility and effectiveness of Georg's position; it is his authority, his "version" of his marriage, his friendship, and his filial devotion, which has collapsed. The reality of existence rears up in the shape of his father, rending the fabric of Georg's carefully considered thoughts (the letter writing doubtless symbolizes his belief that he has made sense of his life in words), brushing aside his last few strands of spoken protest, and destroys him.

The truly Kafkaesque quality of this story, in which Kafka for the first time fused the elements of his inspiration—hitherto expressed in fragmentary form—into a perfect whole, is easier to identify than to explain. It lies in the fact that Georg cannot see how monstrous and

[1] *Tagebücher*, 11 February 1913.

absurd his father's "judgment" is. Or rather, he *can* see this, tries to defend himself with some facetious observations, but nevertheless obeys the judgment as though it were—in the words of his own diary entry—"unshakeable." What has collapsed is Georg's bond with commonsense normality; he is drawn by some inexplicable compulsion, which is as unhesitating as love and as irresistible as the urge to create, towards what he partly knows to be monstrous and absurd.

Doubtless it was in some such way that Kafka, who definitely identified his own fate with that of Georg Bendemann, remained neurotically obsessed with his father, his writing, and his fiancée. This similarity with the circumstances of Kafka's life has led critics to interpret the story in biographical terms. There are, however, some particular difficulties of detail involved in doing this; but before we look at these, there is one more general comment that must be made. The most disquieting question presented by "The Judgment" is this: on what grounds does any judgment about what is monstrous and what is normal ultimately rest?

In the first instance, a man's judgments rest on convention, and at a deeper level they rest on faith. At the beginning of the story Georg gives a conventional account of his life to a friend. At the end, his faith in having the friend—that is to say, convention—on his side is shaken. Then psychological insecurities about the nature of his feelings for his parents and his bride drive him to commit suicide, while still mentally in alert possession of his faculties. Such subconscious compulsion, which reason is powerless to resist, is exactly what psychoanalysis regards as neurotic. In this connection two observations of Freud's are pertinent: first, that the private codes of behavior and fantasy in neurotic patients often resemble actual moral codes, religious beliefs, and works of art, but are caricatures of them. Second, that where an obsessional neurosis is shared by a whole community it need no longer be regarded as sick and may very well be accepted as a religion.

In giving this account of the story, we have already come close to saying what the various characters "stand for." We did not quite interpret the friend as "standing for" convention, however, but interpreted rather the psychological importance to Georg of having a friend, and hence of supposing (mistakenly) that he has a friendly relationship with his father through his friend. The psychological relationships within the story are clearer, in fact, than the characters of the persons between whom they exist; indeed, it is uncertainty about the latter that make the former so compelling. Much of Kafka's effect derives from the impossibility of interpreting—in the sense of "referring to an external convention of meaning"—the three main personages.

On the simplest level of biographical interpretation, for instance, Kafka's actual father generally welcomed, rather than resisted, Kafka's marriage plans; and he did not claim (as the father in the story does) that his son's friends were really his own—these Hermann Kafka did dislike. The friend represented in the story, moreover, does not appear to be an intellectual of any kind, as Kafka's few friends actually were; the most that we can be sure of is that he is a not very successful businessman, destined to "irrevocable bachelorhood," and that he is somehow not respectable in the eyes of Georg's fiancée. If the father is a good family man (and has really been a businessman like Kafka's own father, even though not a very efficient one in the son's eyes—another biographical detail that does not "fit"), then his preference *for* the friend over his own son appears to conflict with the fiancée's prejudice *against* Georg's having such disreputable friends. Of course, one may interpret one's way around these difficulties by saying that what the father really wanted was an unmarried son, and that Kafka's "letter to his father" shows how deeply the son felt his father had made it impossible for him to marry. Before venturing onto this uncertain psychological ground, however, one simpler point has to be made.

In the story Georg appears to be a very efficient businessman, and he finds no problem from his point of view about marrying, whatever difficulties there may be in getting his friend, his fiancée, and his father to accept his plans. It is therefore puzzling to see how Kafka can be identified with this character. The only solution is to regard all the characters—including the fiancée, for Felice Bauer (Kafka's fiancée) can scarcely be supposed to have disapproved of Max Brod (Kafka's friend)!— as relationships within Kafka's mind, as projections of different aspects of his own psyche, and not as real people at all, or even as symbols standing for anything outside himself.

Looked at like this, we can say that a *part* of Kafka was conscientious and competent at the office, and did, as we have seen, earnestly plan to marry. But in another part of his mind Kafka had, as it were, emigrated abroad and had only a remote and unsuccessful relationship to business; this part he knew was doomed to "irrevocable bachelorhood," and to imaginative exposure to all kinds of danger. The crucial relationship with the father also becomes intelligible once we regard the old man not as an independent character, but again as part, the profoundest part, of Kafka's psychological makeup.

A glance again at the "letter to his father" will remind us how little it portrays of an objective person (though it pinpoints a few doubtless real characteristics) by comparison with the subtlety of its portrayal of inner tensions within Kafka, who pursues the ramifications of the relationship entirely within his own mind, writing an imaginary answer from his father, then answering that himself, and so on. Similarly, the father in "The Judgment" does not symbolize at all realistically a businessman, or a family man, or any sort of bourgeois moral code or Jewish belief (which Kafka's actual father did perhaps represent for him). But this Kafkaesque father figure may symbolize Kafka's private *relationship* to some or all of these things: his relationship to the sources of his own life, to the inscrutable and frightening fact of being alive, which he—like the rest of us—tried to "cover up" in conventional platitudes, pretending it was normal when deep down he knew it was monstrous and absurd.

The scene of "covering up" is, as every critic has said, the crucial turning point in the story. It is described as being done with blankets because the German word for to "cover up" (*zudecken*) readily—and perhaps basically—suggests the idea of a blanket (*Decke*); and as we have seen, it is by means of this kind of linguistic association and concretization that Kafka's creative mind works. But it is not a real man or literal father that is covered up in any actual bed; it is the "bed" or source of Kafka's creativity which a part of himself tried to smother with conventionality, at this moment in his career when he had become established in his job and considered marrying. The part that was in danger of being smothered, the creative part, in other words, which Kafka knew to be deeply associated with *his* relationship to his father— although Hermann Kafka, the man, was in reality hardly a very inspiring figure—then rose up and "killed" Kafka. The "wound," as he described the experience of writing this story, was mortal. He was now a true writer; and a writer, as Kafka wrote to Max Brod, "dies (or doesn't really live) and is perpetually sorry for himself."

Martin Greenberg

Gregor Samsa and Modern Spirituality

> *The mother follow'd weeping loud,*
> *'O, that I such a fiend should bear!'*—Blake

> *In the Middle Ages it was the temporal which*
> *was the inessential in relation to spirituality;*
> *in the nineteenth century the opposite occurred;*
> *the temporal was primary and the spiritual was*
> *the inessential parasite which gnawed away at*
> *it and tried to destroy it.*—Sartre

"The Metamorphosis" is peculiar as a narrative in having its climax in the very first sentence: "As Gregor Samsa awoke one morning from uneasy dreams he found himself transformed in his bed into a gigantic insect." The rest of the novella falls away from this high point of astonishment in one long expiring sigh, punctuated by three subclimaxes (the three eruptions of the bug from the bedroom). How is it possible, one may ask, for a story to start at the climax and then merely subside? What kind of story is that? The answer to this question is, I think: A story for which the traditional Aristotelian form of narrative (complication and dénouement) has lost any intrinsic necessity and which has therefore evolved its own peculiar form out of the very matter it seeks to tell. "The Metamorphosis" produces its form out of itself. The traditional kind of narrative based on the drama of dénouement—on the "unknotting" of complications and the coming to a conclusion—could not serve Kafka because it is just exactly the absence of dénouement and conclusions that is his subject matter. His story is about death, but

Reprinted from Martin Greenberg, The Terror of Art, *copyright © 1965, 1966, 1968, by permission of Martin Greenberg and Basic Books, Inc., Publishers, New York.*

Martin Greenberg

...metamorphosis' being a
...ourse it is no dream—
...takes his dream as
...circumstances in
..., since his met-
...al) but a reve-
...ll his soul-
...from the
...av-

...rphosis" announces Gregor
...is slow dying. In its move-
...resembles Tolstoy's *Death*
...nst the knowledge of his
...v's work is about death
...n life. Until Ivan Ilyich
...od one and recognizes that it
...been, he cannot accept the knowl-
...he embraces the truth of his life, which is
...uth of death, and discovers spiritual light and life
...a s protagonist also struggles against "the truths of life
...; in Gregor Samsa's case, however, his life is his death and
...e is no salvation. For a moment, it is true, near the end of his long dying, while listening to his sister play the violin, he feels "as if the way were opening before him to the unknown nourishment he craved"; but the nourishment remains unknown, he is locked into his room for the last time and he expires.

What Gregor awakens to on the morning of his metamorphosis is the truth of his life. His ordinary consciousness has lied to him about himself; the explosive first sentence pitches him out of the lie of his habitual self-understanding into the nightmare of truth. "The dream reveals the reality" of his abasement and self-abasement by a terrible metaphor; he is vermin (*Ungeziefer*), a disgusting creature (or rather un-creature) shut out from "the human circle." The poetic of the Kafka story, based on the dream, requires the literal assertion of metaphor; Gregor must literally *be* vermin. This gives Kafka's representation of the subjective reality its convincing vividness. Anything less than metaphor, such as a simile comparing Gregor to vermin, would diminish the reality of what he is trying to represent.[2] Gregor's thinking "What has happened to me?

[1] Tolstoy's short novel was a "great favorite" of Kafka's, so Max Brod reports in a note to the second volume of the *Diaries*. Philip Rahv makes a detailed comparison of *The Trial* with Tolstoy's work in "The Death of Ivan Ilyich and Joseph K." Both stories, he writes, "echo with the Augustinian imprecation, 'Woe unto thee, thou stream of human custom!' "

[2] In the early fragment "Wedding Preparations in the Country,"* Raban compares himself to a beetle (the idea of vermin is not yet explicit). Kafka uses the vermin simile in the long accusatory letter he wrote his father in 1919: In a rebuttal speech that he puts into the latter's mouth, Hermann Kafka compares his son's

*Franz Kafka, *Wedding Preparations* (Ernest Kaiser and Edith Wilkins, trans.) (London: Secker and Warburg Ltd., 1954). [ed. note]

It was no dream," is no contradiction of his
eam but a literal-ironical confirmation of it. Of
o the dreamer. The dreamer, while he is dreaming
real; Gregor's thought is therefore literally true to t
which he finds himself. However, it is also true ironical
amorphosis is indeed no dream (meaning something un
lation of the truth.

What, then, is the truth of Gregor's life? There is first of
destroying job, which keeps him on the move and cuts him off
possibility of real human associations:

> Oh God, he thought, what an exhausting job I've picked on! 1
> eling about day in, day out. It's much more irritating work than doi
> the actual business in the office, and on top of that there's the trouble
> of constant traveling, of worrying about train connections, the bad
> and irregular meals, the human associations that are no sooner struck
> up than they are ended without ever becoming intimate. The devil
> take it all!

Not only is his work lonely and exhausting, it is also degrading. Gregor
fails to report to work once in five years and the chief clerk is at his
home at a quarter past seven in the morning accusing him of neglect of
his business duties, poor work in general and stealing company funds,
and threatening him with dismissal. In the guilt-world that Gregor in-
habits, his missing his train on this one morning retroactively changes
his excellent work record into the very opposite.

> What a fate, to be condemned to work for a firm where the smallest
> omission at once gave rise to the gravest suspicion! Were all employ-
> ees in a body nothing but scoundrels . . . ?

He has been sacrificing himself by working at his meaningless, degrading job so as to pay off an old debt of his parents' to his employer.
Otherwise "I'd have given notice long ago, I'd have gone to the chief
and told him exactly what I think of him." But even now, with the truth
of his self-betrayal pinning him on his back to his bed, he is unable to
claim himself for himself and decide to quit—he must wait "another five
or six years":

---

way of fighting him to that "of vermin, which not only bite but suck blood at the
same time to get their sustenance. . . . You're unfit for life." But of course the letter, in spite of its peculiarities, is a letter and not *Dichtung*, not a story.

> . . . [O]nce I've saved enough money to pay back my parent
> to him—that should take another five or six years—I'll do it w.
> fail. I'll cut myself completely loose then. For the moment, tho.
> I'd better get up, since my train goes at five.

He pretends that he will get up and resume his old life. He will get dressed "and above all eat his breakfast," after which the "morning's delusions" will infallibly be dissipated. But the human self whose claims he always postponed and continues to postpone, is past being put off, having declared itself negatively by changing him from a human into an insect. His metamorphosis is a judgment on himself by his defeated humanity.

Gregor's humanity has been defeated in his private life as much as in his working life. His mother succinctly describes its deathly aridity as she pleads with the chief clerk:

> ". . . [H]e's not well, sir, believe me. What else would make him miss a train! The boy thinks about nothing but his work. It makes me almost cross the way he never goes out in the evenings; he's been here the last eight days and has stayed at home every single evening. He just sits there quietly at the table reading a newspaper or looking through railway timetables. The only amusement he gets is doing fretwork. For instance, he spent two or three evenings cutting out a little picture frame; you would be surprised to see how pretty it is; it's hanging in his room; you'll see it in a minute when Gregor opens the door . . . ."

The picture in the little frame shows a woman in furs "holding out to the spectator a huge fur muff into which the whole of her forearm had vanished"; it is the second object that Gregor's eye encounters when he surveys his room on waking (the first was his collection of samples). Later in the story, when his sister and mother empty his room of its furniture, he defends his "human past" by making his stand on this picture, pressing "himself to the glass, which was a good surface to hold on to and comforted his hot belly." That is about what Gregor's "human past" amounts to: a pin-up.

For most of the story, Gregor struggles with comic-terrible pathos against the metaphor fastened on him. His first hope is that it is all "nonsense." But he cannot tell; the last thing he knows about is himself. So he works himself into an upright position in order to unlock the door, show himself to the chief clerk and his family, and let them decide for him, as he has always let others decide for him:

y were horrified then the responsibility was no longer his and
could stay quiet. But if they took it calmly, then he had no rea-
on either to be upset, and could really get to the station for the
eight o'clock train if he hurried.

The answer that he gets is his mother's swoon, the chief clerk's hurried departure, in silent-movie style, with a loud "Ugh!" and his father's
driving him back "pitilessly," with a newspaper and a walking stick
that menaces his life, into his room—"from behind his father gave him
a strong push which was literally a deliverance and he flew far into the
room, bleeding freely. The door was slammed behind him with the stick,
and then at last there was silence."

This is the first repulse the metamorphosed Gregor suffers in his
efforts to reenter "the human circle." The fact that his voice has al-
tered so that the others can no longer understand what he says, but he
can understand them as well as ever, perfectly expresses the pathos of
one who is condemned to stand on the outside looking in. Although
he must now accept the fact that he has been changed into a monster,
he clings to the illusion that his new state is a temporary one: "he must
lie low for the present and, by exercising patience and the utmost consideration, help the family to bear the inconvenience he was bound to
cause them in his present condition." Like Ivan Ilyich, he wants to believe that his mortal illness is only a "condition."

In Part II we learn about Gregor's all-important relations with his
family. An unambiguous indication already given in Part I is the fact
that he locks his bedroom doors at night "even at home"—a "prudent
habit he had acquired in traveling." Although he is a dutiful, self-sacri-
ficing son, just such a dutiful son as Georg Bendemann, he is as much a
stranger to his family as he is to the world and shuts them out of his
life—he locks them out as much as they lock him in. Concealment, mistrust, and denial mark the relations in the Samsa family. It now turns
out, as Gregor listens at his bedroom door, that some investments had
survived the wreck of Samsa Sr.'s business five years before and had
even increased since then, though he thought his father had been left
with nothing, "at least his father had never said anything to the contrary, and of course he had not asked him directly." Moreover, this sum
had been increased by the unexpended residue of Gregor's earnings, who
"kept only a few dollars for himself." But he buries the rage he feels at
this evidence of the needlessness of his self-sacrifice, as he has always
buried his real feelings:

Gregor nodded his head eagerly, rejoiced at this evidence of unex-

pected thrift and foresight. True, he could really have paid off so
more of his father's debts to the chief with this extra money, an
so brought much nearer the day on which he could quit his job, bu
doubtless it was better the way his father had arranged it.

His parents liked to think that his slaving at his job to support the
family represented no sacrifice of himself—"they had convinced themselves in the course of years that Gregor was settled for life in this firm."
But they were able to convince themselves of this only because he himself cooperated eagerly with them to deny himself. Deception and self-
deception, denial and self-denial now "end in horror." To cap it all, it
turns out that his family did not even need his sacrifice for another
reason: When Gregor ceases to be the breadwinner, father, mother, and
sister all turn to and provide for themselves and the old man is even
rescued in this way from a premature dotage.

The decisive figure in the family for Gregor is his father He sees
him something like Georg Bendemann saw his—as an old man, almost
a doddering old man, and yet strong. This combination of weakness and
strength is signaled in the story's very first words about Samsa Sr.: "at
one of the side doors his father was knocking, gently [*schwach:* weakly],
yet with his fist." The combination is present in the description of the
father's response to Gregor's first breaking out of his bedroom—a "knot-
ted fist" and "fierce expression" go along with tears of helplessness and
humiliation:

> His father knotted his fist with a fierce expression on his face as if
> he meant to knock Gregor back into his room, then looked uncer-
> tainly round the living room, covered his eyes with his hands and
> wept till his great chest [*mächtige Brust*] heaved.

But in spite of his "great chest," in spite of his voice's sounding "no
longer like the voice of one single father" when he drives his son back
into his room, in spite of Gregor's being "dumbfounded at the enormous
size of his shoe soles," the second time his father chases him back into
his room, the elder Samsa, unlike the elder Bendemann, does not loom
large like a Titanic figure. He is powerful, irascible and petulant, but not
mythically powerful. His shoe soles seem "enormous" to his son because
of his insect angle of vision—not because the old man is superhuman but
because the son is less than human. Everything in the story is seen from
Gregor's point of view, the point of view of somebody who has fallen
below the human level.

The father's strength is the ordinary strength of human life, which
has been temporarily dimmed by his business failure and his son's un-

..ral ascendancy as the breadwinner of the family. He does not battle ..son to recover his ascendancy as Bendemann Sr. does in "The Judg-..ient." There is no battle; Gregor cannot "risk standing up to him." The unnatural state of affairs in the Samsa home corrects itself so to speak naturally, by the son's showing forth as what he really is—a parasite that saps the father's and the family's life. A fundamental incompatibility exists between the son and the family, between sickliness and parasitism on the one hand and vigor and independence on the other, between death and life. As the son's life wanes the family's revives; especially the father's flourishes with renewed vigor and he becomes a blustering, energetic, rather ridiculous man—a regular Kafka papa.

From the start Gregor's father deals brutally with him:

> [F]rom the very first day of his new life . . . his father believed only the severest measures suitable for dealing with him.

Indeed he threatens his life: the first time he shoos Gregor back into his room he menaces him with a "fatal blow" from his stick; at his son's second outbreak he gives him a wound from which he never recovers. But though Samsa Sr. throws his son back into his room two out of the three times he breaks out of it, Gregor's banishment from "the human circle" is not a sentence passed on him by his father. Unlike the father in "The Judgment," Samsa Sr. does not stand at the center of the story confronting his son as the lord and judge of his life. He stands with the mother and the sister, opposite the son but to the side; the center of the story is completely occupied by the son. The father affirms the judg-ment passed on Gregor—that he is "unfit for life"—but the judgment is not his; it is Gregor's. At the beginning of the novella, before he is locked in his room by the family as a metamorphosed monster, we see how he has already locked himself in as a defeated human being. Gregor is self-condemned.

At the side of the father stands the mother, gentle ("That gentle voice!"), yet "in complete union with him" against her son. Gregor's monstrousness horrifies her no less than the others and she faints at the sight of him. For the first two weeks she prefers, with the father, not to know how or even if Gregor is fed. "Not that they would have wanted him to starve, of course, but perhaps they could not have borne to know more about his feeding than from hearsay. . . ."—Gregor's struggle, in these words, against the truth is a pathetically ironical statement of it. Frau Samsa pities her son—"he is my unfortunate son"—and understands his plight as illness; the morning of the metamorphosis she sends the daughter for the doctor, while Herr Samsa, characteristically (his son is a recalcitrant creature bent on causing him a maximum of annoyance, sends the maid for the locksmith. (Gregor, feeling "himself drawn once more into the human circle" by these steps, "hoped for great and remarkable results from both the doctor and the locksmith, without really distinguishing precisely between them"—agreeing with both parents, he is unable to distinguish between the element of recalcitrance and refusal and the element of illness in his withdrawal into inhuman isolation). Shame and horror, however, overwhelm the mother's compassion—we learn from Gregor's reflections that the doctor was sent away on some pretext. She protests against Grete's clearing the furniture out of Gregor's room—". . . doesn't it look as if we were showing him, by taking away his furniture, that we have given up hope of his ever getting better . . . ?" —but then acquiesces weakly in it and even helps to move the heavy pieces. At the end, when Grete says that the bug must be got rid of:

> "He must go," cried Gregor's sister, "that's the only solution, Father. You must try to get rid of the idea that this is Gregor. . . . If this were Gregor, he would have realized long ago that human beings can't live with such a creature, and he'd have gone away on his own accord. . . ."

the mother, with a terrible silence, acquiesces again in her daughter's determination, which this time is a condemnation of her son to death.

Gregor cherishes his sister most of all. She in turn shows the most awareness of his needs after his metamorphosis into vermin and he is grateful to her for it. But he notices that she avoids touching anything that has come into contact with him and he is forced to "realize how repulsive the sight of him still was to her, and that it was bound to go on being repulsive." For her, too, he is a pariah, a monster shut out of the human circle, and at the end she is the one who voices the thought, which has hung unexpressed over the family since the morning of the metamorphosis, that Gregor must be got rid of.

This, then, is the situation in the Samsa family revealed by the metamorphosis: on the surface, the official sentiments of the parents and the sister toward Gregor, and of Gregor toward them and toward himself; underneath, the horror and disgust, and self-disgust: ". . . family duty required the suppression of disgust and the exercise of patience, nothing but patience."

Gregor breaks out of his room the first time hoping that his transformation will turn out to be "nonsense"; the second time, in the course of defending at least his hope of returning to his "human past." His third eruption, in Part III, has quite a different aim. The final section of

e story discovers a Gregor who tries to dream again, after a long inter-
val, of resuming his old place at the head of the family, but the figures
from the past that now appear to him—his boss, the chief clerk, traveling
salesmen, a chambermaid ("a sweet and fleeting memory"), and so on—
cannot help him, "they were one and all unapproachable and he was
glad when they vanished." Defeated, he finally gives up all hope of returning to the human community. Now his existence slopes steeply
toward death. The wound in his back, made by the apple his father threw
at him in driving Gregor back into his room after his second outbreak,
has begun to fester again; his room is now the place in which all the
household's dirty old decayed things are thrown, along with Gregor, a
dirty old decayed thing; and he has just about stopped eating.

At first he had thought he was unable to eat out of "chagrin over the
state of his room"—his mood at that stage of his dying, like Ivan Ilyich's
at a corresponding stage, was one of hatred toward his family for neglect-
ing him; he hissed at them all in rage. But then he discovered that he got
"increasing enjoyment" from crawling about the filth and junk—it was
not the filthiness of his room that was preventing him from eating. On
the last evening of his life, watching from his room the lodgers whom
his family have taken in putting away a good supper, he comes to a
crucial realization:

> "I'm hungry enough," said Gregor sadly to himself, "but not for
> that kind of food. How these lodgers are stuffing themselves, and
> here am I dying of starvation!"

In giving up at last all hope of reentering the human circle, Gregor
finally understands the truth about his life; which is to say he accepts
the knowledge of his death, for the truth about his life is his death-in-life
by his banishment and self-banishment from the human community.
But having finally accepted the truth, having finally bowed to the yoke
of the metaphor that he has been trying to shake off, he begins to sense
a possibility that exists for him *only* in his outcast state. He is hungry
enough, he realizes, but not for the world's fare, "not for that kind of
food." He feels a hunger that can only be felt in full acceptance of his outcast state. Like Ivan Ilich when he accepts his death at last and plunges
into the black sack's hole, he perceives a glimmer of light; in the degra-
dation, in the utter negativity of his outcastness, he begins to apprehend
a positive possibility.

He has already had a hint or two that the meaning of his metamorphosis contains some sort of positive possibility. At the beginning of the
story, when he is lying in bed and worrying about not reporting to

work, he thinks of saying he is sick, but knows that the sick-insurance doctor will come down on him as a malingerer. "And would he be so far from wrong on this occasion? Gregor really felt quite well . . . and he was even unusually hungry." He has just been changed into a huge bug and he is afraid of pleading sick because he will be accused of malingering! And the accusation would after all be correct because he felt quite well and was even unusually hungry! "Of course," the reader says, "he means quite well *as an insect!*"—which is a joke, but a joke that points right to the positive meaning of his metamorphosis.

A second hint soon follows. After Gregor unlocks the bedroom door with his jaws and drops on his legs for the first time, he experiences "a sense of physical comfort; his legs had firm ground under them; . . . they even strove to carry him forward in whatever direction he chose; and he was inclined to believe that a final relief from all his sufferings was at hand." The first meaning here is ironical and comic: Gregor, unable to accept his transformation into a bug and automatically trying to walk like a man, inadvertently falls down on his insect legs and feels an instantaneous sense of comfort which he takes as a promise of future relief from his sufferings. With supreme illogic he derives a hope of release from his animal condition from the very comfort he gets by adapting himself to that condition—so divided is his self-consciousness from his true self. But there is a second meaning, which piles irony upon the irony: *precisely* as a noisome outcast from the human world Gregor feels the possibility of relief, of *final* relief. *Only* as an outcast does he sense the possibility of an ultimate salvation rather than just a restoration of the *status quo*.

As a bug, too, his wounds heal a lot faster than did his old cut finger: the vitality possible to him in his pariah state (if he can only find the food he needs to feed his spiritual hunger on, for he is "unusually hungry") is in sharp contrast with his human debility. And he finds a kind of freedom in crawling around the walls and ceiling of his room instead of going to work each morning—Kafka dwells so much in the first part on the horror of Samsa's job that we feel his metamorphosis as something of a liberation, although in the end he is only delivered from the humiliation and death of his job into the humiliation and death of his outcast state.

When Gregor breaks out of his room the third and last time, he is no longer trying to deceive himself about himself and get back to his old life with its illusions about belonging to the human community. He is trying to find that "final relief" which lies beyond "the last earthly frontier," a frontier which is to be approached only through exile and solitude. What draws him out of his room the last night of his life is his sister's violin playing. Although he had never cared for music in his human state, now the notes of the violin attract him surprisingly. Indifferent to "his growing lack of consideration for the others"—at last he has the courage to think about himself—trailing "fluff and hair and remnants of food" which he no longer bothers to scrape off himself, the filthy starving underground creature advances onto "the spotless floor of the living room" where his sister is playing for the three lodgers.

> Was he an animal, that music had such an effect upon him? He felt as if the way were opening before him to the unknown nourishment he craved.

It is a familiar Romantic idea that Kafka is making use of here: that music expresses the inexpressible, that it points to a hidden sphere of spiritual power and meaning. It is only in his extremity, as "an animal," an outcast from human life who finally accepts his being cast out, that Gregor's ears are opened to music. Yet in spite of all the hints he has had, Gregor still hesitates to grasp the positive possibility contained in the truth about himself and his death in life—the possibility of life in death, of spiritual life through outcastness. All along he has understood the wellbeing he feels as an insect as an indication of his bestialization. "Am I less sensitive now?" he asks himself after marveling at his recuperative powers as a bug; he accuses himself of a growing lack of consideration for others, and so on. Now he does the same thing: "Was he an animal, that music had such an effect upon him?" This time, however, his understanding of himself is clearly a misunderstanding; it is nonsensical to associate music and bestiality, music is at the opposite pole from bestiality. His metamorphosis is a path to the spiritual rather than the bestial. The violin notes that move him so build a way through his death in life to the salvation for which he blindly hungers.

Or they only seem to. Certainly the unknown nourishment exists; the goal of his hunger exists. But the music merely draws him toward his sister with the jealous intention of capturing her for himself and immuring her in his cell with him; it only leads him out into the same old living room of his death as a private person, which with the three indignant lodgers staring down at him is the same old public world of bullying businessmen he knew as a traveling salesman. "There is a goal, but no way," Kafka says in one of his aphorisms; "what we call a way is only wavering."

His final repulse follows, with his sister demanding that "he must go. . . . If this were Gregor, he would have realized long ago that human beings can't live with such a creature. . . ." Painfully turning around,

Gregor crawls back into his room without his father's having to chase him back and surrenders his life to this demand:

> "And what now?" said Gregor to himself, looking round in the darkness. . . . He thought of his family with tenderness and love. The decision that he must disappear was one that he held to even more strongly than his sister, if that were possible. In this state of vacant and peaceful meditation he remained until the tower clock struck three in the morning. The first broadening of light in the world outside the window entered his consciousness once more. Then his head sank to the floor of its own accord and from his nostrils came the last faint flicker of his breath.

Both Georg Bendemann and Gregor Samsa die reconciled with their families in a tenderness of self-condemnation. But Georg is sentenced to death by his father; nobody sentences Gregor to his death in life except himself. His ultimate death, however, his death without redemption, is from hunger for the unknown nourishment he needs. What kills Gregor is spiritual starvation—"Man cannot live without a permanent trust in something indestructible in himself, and at the same time that indestructible something as well as his trust in it may remain permanently concealed from him."

Although the story does not end with Gregor's death, it is still from his point of view that the last few pages are narrated. The family are of course glad to be freed of the burden and scandal he has been to them but dare not say so openly. When the tough old charwoman who has survived "the worst a long life could offer" spares them the embarrassment of getting "rid of the thing," their thanks is to fire her. However, the tide of life, now flooding in, soon sweeps them beyond bad conscience and troubled reflections. They make a holiday of Gregor's death day and take a trolley ride into the country. Spring is in the air; a review of their prospects shows them to be "not at all bad." Mother and father notice how their daughter, in spite of everything, has

> bloomed into a pretty girl with a good figure. They grew quieter and half unconsciously exchanged glances of complete agreement, having come to the conclusion that it would soon be time to find a good husband for her. And it was like a confirmation of their new dreams and excellent intentions that at the end of their journey their daughter sprang to her feet first and stretched her young body.

Life triumphs blatantly, not only over Gregor's unlife but over his posthumous irony—these last lines are entirely without irony. Or if they are ironical it is at Gregor's expense: his moral condemnation of his family here turns into a condemnation of himself. Kafka got his peroration from a description of Ivan Ilyich's daughter in Tolstoy's story, only he twists its meaning right around:

> His daughter came in all dressed up, with much of her young body naked, making a show of it, while his body was causing him such torture. She was strong and healthy, evidently very much in love, and annoyed that his illness and suffering and death should cast a shadow upon her happiness.

Tolstoy's condemnation of the living, with their vulgar bursting vitality and impatience to get on with their business of living forever, in Kafka's hands becomes life's impatient condemnation of the dead that is the novella's last word: "We are sinful not merely because we have eaten of the Tree of Knowledge, but also because we have not yet eaten of the Tree of Life. The state in which we find ourselves is sinful, quite independent of guilt."

Tolstoy's story is dramatic, with a reversal (peripety) and a dénouement at the end in which the dying man finds salvation and death is no more. In Kafka's story there is the beginning of a reversal when Gregor thinks the way to unknown nourishment is opening before him, but it fails to take place and the novella sinks to the conclusion that has been implicit from the start. Kafka's story has little drama; a climax that occurs in the first sentence is no real climax. At the beginning of the chapter I described this nondramatic movement of "The Metamorphosis" as a dying fall, a sinking, an ebbing. *The Trial* and *The Castle* too have more or less the same movement, and in his diary entry of December 13, 1914, Kafka remarks on this dying movement of his best work:

> . . . [T]he best things I have written have their basis in this capacity of mine to die contentedly. All these fine and very convincing passages always deal with the fact that somebody is dying, that it is hard for him to do, that it seems unjust to him or at least cruel, and the reader finds this moving or at least I think he should. For me, however, who believe that I'll be able to lie contentedly on my deathbed, such descriptions are secretly a game, I positively enjoy my own death in the dying person's, therefore I calculatingly exploit the attention that the reader concentrates on death, understand it a lot more clearly than he, who I assume will complain on his deathbed, and for these reasons my complaining [*Klage*, lament] is as perfect as can be, doesn't suddenly break off in the way real complaining

is likely to do, but dies away beautifully and purely. It is the same thing as my always complaining to my mother about pains that weren't nearly as bad as my complaints made one think.

The passage is a characteristically ambivalent appreciation and depreciation of his art for the very same reasons. On the side of depreciation, he suggests that his stories aren't real stories at all, with the dramatic conflict of real stories, but a "game" he plays with the reader: behind the apparent struggle of his protagonists to live, undermining and betraying it from the start, is his own secret embrace of death. And just because the struggle is a fake one he is able to prolong it artfully into a sort of swan song, a swan song which at the end of the diary entry he compares to his hypochondriacal complainings to his mother, to his constant whinings about aches and pains. In this Kafka seems to be agreeing with those critics who find him a pusillanimous neurotic, lacking in any force or fight. Edmund Wilson thinks he is "at his most characteristic when he is assimilating men to beasts—dogs, insects, mice, and apes—which can neither dare nor know . . . . the denationalized, discouraged, disaffected, disabled Kafka . . . can in the end only let us down." A psychoanalytic critic concludes that "the striving for synthesis, for integration and harmony which are the marks of a healthy ego and a healthy art are lacking in Kafka's life and in his writings. The conflict is weak in Kafka's stories because the ego is submissive; the unequal forces within the Kafka psyche create no tension within the reader, only a fraternal sadness . . . ."

But on the side of appreciation, Kafka sees his understanding of death as being responsible for his "best things." Thanks to his underlying acceptance of death, the selfsame story that he is always telling about somebody who finds it hard to die is "as perfect as can be" and "dies away beautifully and purely."

Which is it then? Is "The Metamorphosis" unhealthy art—the artfully prolonged whine of a disaffected neurotic with a submissive ego? Or is it a lament (*Klage*) that is perfect, beautiful, pure? Does Kafka let us down in the end or does he try to lift us up "into the pure, the true, the unchangeable"? The two opposing characterizations, "neurotic whine" and "beautiful lament," which I have drawn from Kafka's diary entry express very different judgments, but they agree in pointing to something lyrical about the form of his "best things," something in the nature of a crying-out, rather than a narrative of action with complication and dénouement. Doubtless Kafka's critics would find him depressing in any case. Yet in taxing his stories with lack of tension they misunderstand their form and ask them to be what they are not and do not try to be—representations of action. And in missing their form they miss the meaning—these stories do not mean the unmanliness and discouragement of their protagonists; they mean the courage to see the unmanliness and discouragement which live like an infection at the heart of modern spirituality, perhaps even, as Kafka wrote to Milena Jesenská, at the heart of "all faith since the beginning of time."

"The Metamorphosis" does not unfold an action but a metaphor; it is the spelling out of a metaphor. It does not end in an Aristotelian dénouement, but draws the metaphor out to its ultimate conclusion which is death. I called the movement of the story a dying fall. But visual terms serve better than auditory ones. The movement is a seeing more and more: waking up, the metamorphosed Gregor sees his insect belly, then his helplessly waving legs, then his room, cloth samples, picture, alarm clock, furniture, key, living room, family, chief clerk—on and on in a relentless march of ever deeper seeing till he sees his own death. Everything he sees is a building stone added to the structure of the metaphor of his banishment from the human circle, capped by the stone of his death. In a story of this kind there is no question of tension or of any of the specifically dramatic qualitites: it is a vision.

Of course Gregor Samsa "can neither dare nor know." Neither can Hamlet, his ultimate literary ancestor and the earliest protagonist of the modern theme of doubt and despair in face of the threat of universal meaninglessness. That is just the point of the story: Gregor can neither dare nor know, neither live in the world nor find the unknown truth he craves.

Heinz Politzer

Parable and Paradox: *"In the Penal Colony"*

Next to "The Metamorphosis," "In the Penal Colony" is the longest short story Kafka wrote during his best years. It is also outwardly the most conclusive. Although it was written in 1914, it was not published until 1919. In its center emerges another "thing," an execution machine. The first sentence of the story introduces the machine as "a peculiar piece of apparatus," a formidable understatement indeed. Although this device is as dead as it is deadly, its presence so dominates the story that the human figures around it must be relegated to minor roles; they are not even accorded the privilege of having proper names.

The machine sits in a deep hollow surrounded on all sides by bare slopes which isolate it even from the rest of this small island, the site of a Penal Colony for an unidentified but unmistakably European power. The machine itself, in its slow, meticulous execution of the detailed instructions given it, suggests the inevitability of fate. The lunar landscape surrounding it and the sea cutting off the island from the civilized world fortify this impression.

The apparatus seems to rise from the interior of the earth; at the same time it points to the "glare of sunshine poured out" over the valley, so that its parts "almost flash out rays." Actually and metaphorically depth and height are united in this death-dealing contraption. It consists of three parts: the Bed, the Harrow, and the Designer. An officer, who appears to be the master as well as the servant of the machine, explains its function with passionate detachment:

> On the bed here the condemned man is laid, . . . face down, quite naked, . . . here are straps for the hands, here for the feet, and here

the neck, to bind him fast. Here at the head of the bed . . . is
nis little gag of felt, which . . . is meant to keep him from screaming
and biting his tongue. Of course the man is forced to take the felt
into his mouth, for otherwise his neck would be broken by the
strap. . . . Both the Bed and the Designer have an electric battery; the
Bed needs one for itself, the Designer for the Harrow. As soon as the
man is strapped down, the Bed is set in motion, . . . the movements
are all precisely calculated, . . . they have to correspond precisely to
the movements of the Harrow, . . . the shape of the Harrow corresponds to the human form; here is the harrow for the torso, here are
the harrows for the legs. For the head there is only this one small
pike. . . . When the man lies down on the Bed and it begins to vibrate,
the Harrow is lowered onto his body. . . . As it quivers, its points
pierce the skin of the body which is itself quivering from the vibra-
tion of the Bed. So that the actual progress . . . can be watched, the
Harrow is made of glass . . . . In the Designer are all the cogwheels
which control the movements of the Harrow, and this machinery is
regulated according to the inscription demanded by the sentence. . . .
Whatever commandment the prisoner has disobeyed is written upon
his body by the Harrow.

Taken by itself, the machine is a very simple device: it communicates
the guilt of the accused to him by engraving it into his flesh. A popular
German adage says: "He who refuses to hear must feel," feel the pain
of punishment. Moreover, there exists an etymological connection between "hearing," "listening," and "obeying" *(hören, horchen,* and
gehorchen) so that Kafka could rely on his German readers to understand
intuitively the meaning of his machine: he who disobeyed was bound to
feel the consequences on his own body. Translating a proverb into an
image, Kafka followed an old convention related to the technique of the
fable. Pieter Brueghel used a similar technique when he painted adages
current in the Netherlands of his time and filled them with a strange,
half-allegorical, half-realistic life. In Kafka's own time European children
were still fond of acting charades, which often represented proverbs by
living figures, whose message was to be guessed by the onlookers.

Ostensibly the execution is as uncomplicated as the machine. The
torture is scheduled to last for twelve hours. (We may note here another
appearance of the mystic number twelve. It is in accord with his previous
uses of this number to suppose that Kafka intends the twelve hours of
punishment to represent an eternity of torture.) "During the first six
hours the condemned man lives almost as before, he only suffers pain."
Kafka is true to his masochistic view of life when he minimizes the
importance of physical suffering. For the condemned man the turning
point arrives about the sixth hour, when "insight dawns upon the most
stupid. . . . Nothing more happens than that the man begins to under-

stand the inscription, he purses his mouth as if he were listening." This is, of course, the time when the needles of the Harrow have sunk deep enough into his flesh to start the actual killing. Insight and death are interdependent; together they form the "work" which is to be "completed" during the second six hours. During this time a "look of transfiguration" appears on the face of the sufferer, and the spectators of the execution can now "bathe [their] cheeks in the radiance of a justice which was achieved at long last and was already beginning to fade away." At the end of the period the corpse is automatically cast into a pit, whereupon it is buried.

The simplicity of this machine and its workings is deceptive and proves to be superficial as soon as one questions its purpose. Although the dying man seems to be listening at long last, he is given no chance to obey the command which has reached him too late. He is allowed no second thought, given no opportunity to regret and repent. Without regard for the gravity of his crime a sentence of death is proclaimed as his only means of atonement. Not even the argument most frequently used by the advocates of capital punishment can be said to apply here; the death inflicted by this machine does not serve to deter others from crime. Far from being a grave and ominous event, the execution assumes the character of a popular rally with a definitely festive air; small children are assigned the most favorable locations to "bathe" in this spectacle as if it were the source of a miraculous power. The revelation of a supranatural force seems to appear in the death pangs of the executed man and to vanish as *rigor mortis* freezes his face. There is a certain similarity between the thing Odradek* and the execution machine; although both are described realistically in great detail and with much ironic gusto, both serve as messengers from a world far beyond any reality we know.

The mystery expressed by the execution machine is the mystery of the law. As will be seen, this obvious link between "In the Penal Colony" and *The Trial* is more than a superficial one. The law which is executed by the machine has its foundation in a logic well outside the patterns of civilized justice. It seems to us an unjust law, but actually it is related to the justice practiced by primitive tribes and martial courts. Accordingly it is a very primitive verdict that is about to be written into the body of the sinner before us: "Honor your superior." But this primitiveness is just as deceptive as the simplicity of the machine itself. The paradox of this brand of justice is revealed as soon as we consider the question of the guilt which provoked this judgment.

---

*Odradek is a strangely-shaped messenger from an unreal world imposed upon the family man's reality in "The Worries of a Family Man." It does not live, nor is it able to die [ed. note].

The culprit is a private soldier assigned to a Captain. He must serve his superior both as an orderly and as a servant. It seems that he has to perform the latter duties during the day, the former at night. At night he must get up every hour and salute the Captain's door. Apart from the blatant uselessness of this routine, it robs him of the sleep necessary to allow him to satisfy his master during the day. Yet he "must be alert in both functions." Consequently, the unfortunate private, "a stupid-looking, wide-mouthed creature with matted hair and bewildered face," has taken the line of least resistance to solve this dilemma: he is found asleep on his master's doorstep when the Captain makes a random check. The superior disciplines him on the spot. Thereupon the soldier catches hold of the officer's legs, crying: "Throw your whip away or I'll devour you." The threat of the insurgent is just as self-contradictory as the offense of which he has been accused: he menaces his master with destruction and yet he remains squatting on the floor. How else could he have shaken the legs of the Captain? The Captain consequently does not take the menace seriously; he simply reports the incident to *his* superior, the officer in charge of the Penal Colony and the execution machine. "The Captain came to see me an hour ago," the officer explains; "I wrote down his statement and appended the sentence to it." There is to be no hearing. "If I had first called the man before me and interrogated him, only confusion would have ensued. He would have told lies, and had I succeeded in exposing these lies, he would have made up for them by new lies, and so forth." To the question "Does he know his sentence?" the answer is given: "There would be no point in telling him. He will learn it on his own body." Clarity, straightforwardness, elimination of possible mistakes, dispersion of all and sundry doubts, distinguish this process of law. "That was all quite simple," the officer sums up.

The monolithic simplicity of this system of justice rests on the basic assumption that "guilt is never to be doubted." The officer's guiding principle is echoed later in *The Trial* by the assertion of Titorelli, the court painter, that he had never once experienced a single acquittal. The Prison Chaplain who remarks in the Cathedral scene of *The Trial* that his court's "proceedings . . . gradually merge into the verdict" might just as well be talking about the Penal Colony and its law-enforcing apparatus. K.'s retort to Titorelli, "One single executioner could replace the whole law court," takes form in the figure of the officer who serves the Penal Colony simultaneously as judge, jailer, and hangman. In the second sentence of this tale the reader is informed of the accusation; its wording is made known to him in no uncertain terms; he is left to wonder only at the absurd conditions that brought about this action and at the frightening effectiveness of its execution. The verdict of the machine, with its individual message for each victim despite a common manner of execution, corresponds to the door in the parable "Before the Law," which, although intended for only a single individual, leads to a law assumed to be universal.

"In the Penal Colony" and *The Trial* are closely related by their conception of the paradoxical nature of law. They are, however, sharply distinguished from one another by the fact that K.'s guilt in *The Trial* remains unknown, whereas the soldier's offense in this story is more than clearly stated. Since "In the Penal Colony" and *The Trial* are in this way complementary, we may derive from the soldier's guilt certain conclusions concerning the guilt of Joseph K. in the novel. K.'s crime may have been to disobey a self-contradictory demand of a very general nature. Like the soldier, K. may have been expected to do more than he could possibly perform in his simple middle-class world; like the soldier's guilt, his crime may also reflect the primitive cruelty of the authorities persecuting him.

In the novel it is Joseph K. who doubts the system of law which persecutes him. The inarticulate half-wit in the short story could not be entrusted with an intellectual task of this magnitude. Therefore Kafka has provided a doubter in the person of the Explorer who chances upon the soldier's execution and eventually rescues him, seemingly also by chance. Although nameless like the condemned man, he is more readily accessible to the reader's mind. At times he even appears to function as the narrator's double; on the surface the story is told from a point of view only slightly removed from the attitudes and opinions of the traveler. And yet Kafka can be identified as little—and as much—with this Explorer as he is with his antagonist, the officer; he hides behind them and gains many an ironical twist from the distance which still separates him from both figures.

The traveler is a European, and his mind is conditioned by a civilization beyond the sea. He travels "only as an observer," though he presents himself as a man of considerable social, perhaps even political, influence. For he "had recommendations from high quarters, had been received (in the Colony) with great courtesy, and the very fact that he had been invited to attend the execution seemed to suggest that his views would be welcome." Although he is firmly resolved to use the visitor's prerogative and remain aloof, come what may, he cannot deny from the very beginning "the injustice of the procedure and the inhumanity of the execution." He is gradually drawn into the proceedings, ironically for no other reason than that he is an outsider and therefore a disinterested party. Precisely because he is "conditioned" by European ideas, he is called upon to pronounce judgment upon the machine and the legal system it represents. And since he is "basically honest and unafraid," he condemns the machine with the self-assurance of a man nurtured by tolerance and humanitarianism.

His judgment in turn shatters the basis on which the machine and the law of the Penal Colony are constructed. With the cryptic words, "Then the time has come," the officer sets the condemned man free and proceeds to sacrifice himself in his stead. This sacrificial death ruins the machine.

> The teeth of a cogwheel showed themselves and rose higher, soon the whole wheel was visible, it was as if some enormous force were squeezing the Designer so that there was no longer room for this wheel, the wheel moved up till it came to the very edge of the Designer, fell down, rolled along the sand a little, stood upright on its rim and then lay flat. But a second wheel was already after it.

In the hour of its destruction the inhuman machine seems to acquire human life; the wheel stands upright—a feat as unnatural as the upright stance of the thing Odradek; it only loses its "life" when its frame breaks down over the corpse of the officer. With the point of the great iron spike extending from his forehead, the victim fails to show even the slightest trace of the promised redemption. If his death was meant to be a sacrifice, then his offering was not accepted. The words he had instructed the Designer to imprint upon his body were: "Be just!" The officer's death and the breakdown of the machine together mark the termination of the reign of justice as the officer understood it.

This machine, whose composition and decomposition are described with equal perspicuity and love, is Kafka's prime symbol during these years. If his purpose was to concentrate in one universally valid image the process of dehumanization characteristic of the time of the First World War, then he found it here in this symbol of man's self-destructive ingenuity. If he sought to make externally manifest the hidden legal process of _The Trial,_ then he found his symbol in this "peculiar piece of apparatus." If, finally, he attempted to catch a glimpse of a transcendent existence behind the rationalized and organized reality of twentieth-century civilization, then his invention of a machine which combined the streamlined glamor of technology with the barbarous primitiveness of a divinely justified martial law was a real stroke of genius. Here, too, the mysterious penetrates the world of experience solely in order to pronounce its principal taboo: "Do not enter." But even the destruction of this monstrous thing leaves a mark on the civilized earth; even when it has disappeared, its ghost lingers on. It continues to haunt the island and succeeds in putting the Explorer to an ignominious flight.

The execution machine may be understood as an image of the tortures to which Kafka, the writer, subjected himself. Apart from translating a proverb into a symbol, it may also express Kafka's belief that writing, his writing, had a deadly quality. When the officer spreads out the sheet of paper with the instructions for the Designer, the Explorer is unable to see anything on it but "a labyrinth of lines crossing and re-crossing each other, which covered the paper so thickly that it was difficult to discern the blank spaces between them." This is an accurate description of Kafka's own manuscript pages, which resemble hieroglyphics of an unknown language, beautiful and terrifying at the same time. The word "labyrinth" indicates a basic structural design that Kafka has used as a ground plan for many of his works, especially, as we shall see, for *The Castle*. The two commands the Designer inscribes— "Honor your superior" and "Be just"—are exactly the orders to which Kafka, the metaphysical anarchist, and his main figures give perpetual offense. The word Designer (*Zeichner*) is itself ambiguous; the verdict it designs can also be understood as the basic design of many of Kafka's own writings, quite apart from the innumerable drawings (*Zeichnungen*) with which Kafka adorned the margins of his manuscripts, cryptic ciphers of the message which the writer knew very well he could not convey by words alone.

The Explorer can admit only that this "labyrinth of lines" is "very artistic" (*sehr kunstvoll*), when he is asked his opinion about the *judgment* in this particular *trial* (throughout "In the Penal Colony" Kafka alludes to these themes and titles). Being honest, the Explorer adds, "But I cannot make it out." Here Kafka seems to touch upon the inherent difficulty any esoteric work of literature—and certainly his own—holds for its readers. (The word "deadly," so appropriately describing the script of the Designer, may have been repeated by Kafka, when in sinister moods he passed judgment on his writings.) For the initiated the meaning is obvious—what could be simpler to understand than the command "Honor your superior!" inscribed upon a lazy mutineer? For the outsider it remains unintelligible, unreadable, and thoroughly confusing. The officer experiences as reality what for the Explorer is at best a successful artifice. In other words, the officer still belongs to a system of belief—whatever the merits of this system and the creed of this belief may be; the Explorer, a child of the enlightenment, can only see but does not believe. The difficulty that Kafka's writings, and "In the Penal Colony" in particular, offer the reader stems from the fact that Kafka himself has taken a stand somewhere between the officer and the Explorer.

Unlike Kafka's writings, the script used by the Designer contains an unambiguous message. But this message points parabolically beyond itself into regions beyond reality. Literally these regions open only to him who is forced to leave reality, that is, to die. "Yes," answers the officer, "it is no calligraphy for schoolchildren. You have to keep reading it a long time. . . . Of course the script must not be simple; it is not meant to kill a man straight off." The condemned man is not allowed to penetrate the mystery of the written word until his spirit is about to leave his body. "The spirit becomes free only when it ceases to be a support," Kafka noted in his "Reflections." Ironically, it may be added, the moment of insight and "transfiguration" arrives only when the eyes fail. The spiritual freedom Kafka contemplated was a freedom *from* the body and its reality. If, as Brod maintains, Kafka was a figure "pointing the way," then the way he pointed had to cross the valley of death before it could reach the heights of freedom. At least this was the mystique to which he subscribed in 1913 when he entered in his diary: "The immense world I have in my head. But how to free myself and free it without being torn to pieces. And a thousand times better to be torn to pieces than retain it in me or bury it. This, indeed, is why I am here." That the task he performed was a deadly one became apparent to the writer during his working hours, which were spent, as he said, "with . . . a complete opening of the body and the soul." In these hours of ecstatic agony he resembled the victim at the mercy of a torture machine. On August 6, 1914, he wrote:

> Thus I waver, continually fly to the summit of the mountain, but can hardly maintain myself up there for a moment. Others waver too, but in lower regions, with greater strength; if they are in danger of falling, they are caught by a kinsman who walks beside them for this very purpose. But I waver up there; it is not death, alas, but the eternal torments of dying.

Struggling between life and death, he also experienced the mystical transfiguration of the dying victim. More than once he mentions the sensation of a "great fire," in which even "the strangest fancies . . . perish and are resurrected" and he himself soars "carrying [his] own weight on his back" and moves "as if [he] were advancing in water." In his own body he reenacted the rituals of creation and creator's self-sacrifice, both of which were as tormenting as they were inspiring.

The script of the Designer is certainly more than a code for Kafka's literary work. The German word *Schrift* connotes both "script" and "writing"; it also stands for the Holy Scriptures. Toward the end of his life Kafka said to Gustav Janouch: "It is not by chance that the Bible is called the Scriptures (*die Schrift*)." Accordingly he created in the torture machine of "In the Penal Colony" a metaphor of what religion meant to him. To be sure, writing appeared to him as "a form of prayer." But this description takes account of the human attitude only. It is the metaphysical side—the answer, as it were, which man's prayer could expect to be given—that he referred to in the following aphorism: "A belief like a guillotine—as heavy, as light." Pointedly Kafka uses here the indefinite article, *a* belief. For it was not belief in general but only a particular form of it which he likened to a cold and mechanical instrument of death. Unfortunately this particular form of belief was his. Heavy and difficult (*schwer*) before the believer becomes completely aware of the deadly judgment, it becomes easy (*leicht*) afterward when the blades of the guillotine or the Harrow of the torturing machine have done their duty and the victim's spirit is freed from the body it previously had to support. The "labyrinth of lines" which contains the judgment has reminded many a reader of a page printed in Hebrew, just as the grave and final cadence of the officer's commandments may have been borrowed from the Decalogue. But Kafka is far from equating the torture machine with Jewish belief. This is clear if only for so simple a reason as that its purpose radically contradicts the ethic of the Sixth Commandment: "Thou shall not kill." The paradoxical character of this image consists in the fact that it expresses only a belief, a way of writing, a personal conflict, and yet seems to possess a parabolical, that is, universal, validity. Instead of showing man as a killer of God, it represents God as a hunter and slayer of men.

In its primitiveness the torture machine points to an archaic stage of religious development. This stage appears, in the mind of the officer, as the golden age of the human race, an epoch of superhuman order imposed upon a world guilty by its very existence. No bond or covenant could possibly be concluded between this law and mankind. Instead their relation was one of magic. The Bed of the torture machine is an altar, on which a man is slaughtered in honor of the monstrous idol, Law. If the idol is merciful—and it seems to have been merciful in the past whenever its appetite was sated—it performed a miracle in return and transfigured the victim. In spite of its mechanical sophistication the apparatus seems to be a relic from the times of primordial savagery. Its destruction appears as the precondition for the dawning of a new age, which is more human as well as more rational.

But appearances in Kafka are deceptive. The Penal Colony was the work of the old Commandant, a legendary figure who invented the machine and even drew the patterns for the Designer. We need not stray too far afield from Kafka's intentions to call the old Commandant the Archdesigner. "Did he combine everything in himself?" asks the incredulous Explorer. "Was he soldier, judge, mechanic, chemist, and draughtsman?" "Indeed he was," the officer replies without a moment's hesitation. This Commandant, who united in his person the functions of Lord of Hosts, Supreme Judge, and Creator, had died a long time before, leaving responsibility for the machine to the officer. But the officer has been allowed only the burden of the old Commandant's heritage; the authority has passed on to another man. A managerial type, the new Commandant has turned away from the administration of justice, as his predecessor understood it. He has focused his interest on the economic and political rehabilitation of the island and does his best to transform the Penal Colony into a civilian one. With his appearance life on the island has acquired an atmosphere of democratic liberalism. While allowing the machine to disintegrate in its hidden valley, he opens the Colony to the world by improving its port installations. Politically the new Commandant has destroyed the autocratic regime of the old one by appointing a commission of all the senior officers. To his annoyance even the Penal Officer has been made a member of this body. Moreover, the transient visitor from abroad, the Explorer, is expected to express his opinion before this commission, a polite gesture, obviously intended to better public relations and create international good will. The officer cannot help interpreting this diplomatic nicety as a clever move by which the new Commandant intends to undermine his position still further:

> He has calculated it carefully: this is your second day on the island, you did not know the old Commandant and his ways, . . . perhaps you object on principle to capital punishment. . . . Now, taking all this into consideration, would it not be likely (so thinks the Commandant) that you might disapprove of my methods?

Thereupon the officer goes to work on the mind of the Explorer, trying to swing him to his side by brainwashing him. Falling prey to his prejudices and illusions, he finally comes close to seeing in the Explorer a defender of the faith, his own faith, of course. At the end of a tortuous monologue he all but entrusts to the Explorer the final verdict over his system of justice. (With an equally grotesque misjudgment the jackals in "Jackals and Arabs" heap all their grudges and hopes on a traveler from the "far North": "Master, you are the one to end this quarrel which divides the world. . . . And so, master, . . . by means of your all-powerful hands slit the Arabs' throats through with these scissors"! The scissors as an instrument for cleansing the world bear a remarkable similarity to the torture machine as well as to the "guillotine" representing Kafka's belief.)

But the officer's plea for the Explorer's intervention is not only a sign of his utter failure at psychology, it is also a sin against the very system for which he stands. As a matter of course the officer has denied the condemned man all legal assistance and outside help; now, having nonsensically maneuvered himself into the position of a defendant, he clamors for the very help he had refused to grant. Thereby he offends the law under which he has been operating and indicts himself, even before the Explorer—and through him the new Commandant—have rejected the executioner, and with him his system. The commandment "Be just!" through which he dies, can only mean: Be as just unto yourself as you are to others! It is this justice unto himself which the officer practices when he allows himself to be strapped down on the Bed of the machine. The judge has proved to be guilty himself, and the law is forced to turn against its most faithful executioner. With him the law eliminates itself. It is the end of the trial.

And yet this end of the trial indicates neither the end of the law nor the victory of the new era. Kafka carefully keeps his distance from the new Commandant just as he did from the old. The new Commandant never enters the scene. Whatever we learn about him is colored by the officer's irate words. It cannot be denied that he brought a note of moderation to the island as well as introduced a feminine element. Indeed, the new Commandant seems to have surrounded himself with ladies, who follow him wherever he goes, dampen any loud word uttered in his presence, and disturb the execution by stuffing "the condemned man with sugar candy before he is led off." One does not have to be partial to the officer's way of thinking to notice an objective incongruity in his caustic observation that the condemned man "has lived on stinking fish his whole life and now he has to eat sugar candy"! We are, after all, still on a primitive island. Even the officer has begun to succumb to the ladies' luxuriousness; under the collar of his uniform he has tucked two of their delicate handkerchiefs, confiscated from the condemned soldier to whom they had been given first. All this means that the standards on the island have been confused through the ladies' presence. Adoringly they call the new Commandant's voice "a voice of thunder," an attribute incompatible with his mild attitudes and probably borrowed from his gruffly masculine predecessor. By the repeated turn of the phrase, "the Commandant's ladies," the officer furthermore seems to imply the existence of romantic bonds between the new executive and his entourage. Finally there is a fragment belonging to "In the Penal Colony," which shows the new Commandant "blithely" ordering his laborers to prepare the way for the "snake, . . . the great Madame. . . . She is a snake without peer, she has been thoroughly pampered by our labor and by now there is nobody to compare with her. . . . She should call herself Madame at least." Kafka never disclosed what he had in mind when he drafted this obscure alternative to his story. But the snake, whose way the new Commandant was to prepare, inevitably evokes the image of the serpent in the Garden of Eden, whereas "Madame" is a euphemism for the keeper of a brothel. Here as elsewhere in his stories Kafka uses women as symbols to show how the order of the law is being weakened by the temptations of sex. The company he keeps is meant to discredit the new Commandant not only in the eyes of the Explorer but in those of the reader as well. Even if the new Commandant is to remain the Colony's master after the close of the story, the effectiveness of his command has been called in question.

Nor does Kafka take an altogether favorable view of the other exponent of modern civilization, the Explorer. To positivistic readers the Explorer will appear as one of their own. Austin Warren describes him as "a naturalist, a scientist who shares the humanitarian views of his secularist generation but who, as a social scientist, is capable of intellectual curiosity and a suspension of judgment." This "suspension of judgment" seems to have lured the officer into entrusting the Explorer with the final decision in the matter of the machine. In his despair he chooses as his advocate the self-styled spokesman of progressive enlightenment. But on closer examination we see that this does not describe the Explorer altogether accurately. He cannot conceal from himself his ever-growing fascination for the infernal apparatus. At first he is attracted by the technical perfection of the mechanics of the machine. Hardly has the officer begun to demonstrate the instrument when the Explorer feels "a little captivated." When the machinery is tentatively set into motion, he forgets the deadly purpose of this brilliant technical performance. His only annoyance at this point is caused by a disturbance in the wheels: "If the wheel had not creaked, it would have been glorious." When he becomes conscious of the conflict between the "glorious" play of the instrument and the horrifying end served by this play, he settles for a compromise: he remains opposed to the system but admits that he has been "touched" by the "sincere conviction" of the officer. He is determined to preserve his neutrality even when events take an unexpected turn and the officer prepares to take the soldier's place. "He knew very well what was going to happen, but he had no right to obstruct the officer in anything. If the judicial procedure which the officer cherished was really so near its end, . . . then the officer was doing the right thing; in his place the Explorer would not have acted otherwise." Unlike the officer, the Explorer has no absolute norm he feels bound to follow. In a sense deeper than the one suggested by Warren his judgment is indeed suspended; it has no basis and no aim. He decides to let this exotic ritual take its course, all the more so as he sees it as the last of its kind.

Ultimately the Explorer is only a practicing cultural relativist. With the hauteur of the civilized man he observes the behavior pattern of a group of people alien and inferior to his own. What seemed at first to be a deeply felt attitude—his hostility to the machine and the system supporting it—was only a conditioned reflex, the defense mechanism of positivist rationality faced by the archaic and irrational.

The end of the story proves this point, perhaps even too drastically. Followed by the rescued soldier and his guardian, a fellow soldier, the Explorer reaches the beach and starts bargaining with the ferryman to row him to the steamer.

> By the time [the two soldiers] reached the foot of the steps the Explorer was already in the boat, and the ferryman was just casting off from the shore. They could have jumped into the boat, but the Explorer lifted a heavy knotted rope from the floor boards, threatened them with it, and so kept them from attempting the leap.

Since, after all, it is the Explorer who saved the soldier from death, he might be expected to show some signs of enduring interest in him. Now he is offered an opportunity to give concrete proof of the humanitarianism for the sake of which he rejected the machine before. But the Explorer remains unmoved, and by missing this opportunity reveals a sluggishness of heart which parallels the premeditated cruelty expressed by the torture machine; man does not matter in either case. And yet there is a distinction to be made. The mind which devised the machine was a primitive one, still untouched by the idea of humanitarianism. The Explorer, on the other hand, represents the processes of dehumanization which corrodes any civilization in the hour of its decline. Prehumanitarianism and posthumanitarianism meet in this story. The bewildered and wordless human creature, the soldier, is neglected by both.

This Explorer appears as a caricature of twentieth-century materialism: he is indifferent to the drama he happens to have witnessed, dazzled by the achievements of technology without regard for their primitive origins and savage ends, and willing to pay lip service to progressive and liberal ideals but incapable of applying them even to the simplest action. Unlike any other Kafka figure, he is allowed to return home. From the ease with which he refuses help to the survivors of the ghastly scene we can conclude that he will not find it difficult to wipe the nightmare from his memory. For him Western civilization will remain intact in spite of the mechanized barbarism he has experienced somewhere on the fringes of his culture.

Kafka seems to pass judgment on the Explorer during this last scene, but we cannot accept this judgment as final because he was never satisfied with this ending. When, in a letter to Kurt Wolff, he called the last

two or three pages of the story "wretched" (*Machwerk*), he probably
was annoyed at the obviousness of the conclusion: how could he allow
the Explorer to escape? The letter is dated September 4, 1917; less than
a month before he entered in his diary several attempts to continue the
story in a different vein. One of these sketches contains the vision of the
"Great Madame" quoted above; another shows the executed officer,
"the spike protruding from his shattered forehead," as he appears in the
Explorer's imagination, carrying the traveler's baggage. "A conjuring
trick?" the Explorer asks. "No," the ghost officer replies, "a mistake
on your part; I was executed on your command." Here the Explorer is
resolved to report at home what he has seen on the island; he will bear
witness; he betrays sympathy, a tendency Kafka abandoned because it
was neither in conformity with the character of the Explorer nor with the
air of annoyance which, as Kafka knew very well, pervades the whole
story. During the officer's self-execution the traveler found the presence
of the soldier and the guardian annoying. (The German word *peinlich* in-
cludes also the nuance of "painful.") The same word reappears in a letter
to Wolff, who had found fault with "In the Penal Colony" as a whole
on account of its *Peinlichkeit*. "To explain my last story," Kafka wrote,

> I only want to add that it is not unique in being painfully annoying.
> Rather, our time in general and my own time in particular were and
> continue to be likewise very annoying, and my particular time even
> more so than time in general. God knows how deep I would have
> gotten this way if I had continued to write or, better, if my circum-
> stances and my condition had permitted me to write, as I, all my
> teeth buried in all my lips (*sic!*) had wished to do [October 11,
> 1916]!

Had he continued to write, the end would have been even more
excruciating.

Even as the story now stands, it contains intimations of the future
Kafka had in mind for his Penal Colony, and perhaps for the world at
large. Early in his explanations the officer mentions the old Commandant's followers: during his lifetime

> the Colony was full of [them] . . . there are still many left but none
> will admit it. If you were to go to the teahouse today, on execution
> day, and listen around, you would perhaps hear only ambiguous re-
> marks. All of these would be made by partisans, but under the pres-
> ent Commandant and his present doctrines they are of no use to me.

The teahouse is one of "the first houses of the Colony"; it lies between the harbor installations of the new Commandant and the torture

machine of the old. The Explorer stops there on his way to the sea. Being a sensitive observer, he immediately comes under the spell of "historical reminiscences" and feels "the power of past days." He notices the "cool, damp air"—the air of a tomb—which emanates from the interior. Soon he learns that "the old man," that is, the old Commandant, is buried here. He is shown a gravestone hidden under a table. Its inscription reads: "Here rests the old Commandant. His followers, who now must be nameless, have dug this grave and set up this stone. There is a prophecy that after a certain number of years the Commandant will rise again and lead his followers from this house to reconquer the Colony. Have faith and wait!" At first the letters of this inscription are as illegible as the "labyrinth" of the script of the Designer. Only after the Explorer has gone down on his knees is he able to decipher this writing, the last in a story dedicated to the imagery of *Schrift*. Although the Explorer has a perfectly rational excuse for bending his knees, the reader cannot help feeling that here at last he pays his involuntary respect to the spirit of the old Commandant. When he rises up again, the bystanders catch his eyes. They are "poor humiliated folk, . . . strong men with short, glistening, full black beards, . . . probably dock laborers." The Explorer does not hear any of the ambiguous remarks that the officer had predicted, but he notices on their faces a smile, "as if they too had read the inscription, had found it ridiculous and were expecting him to agree with them." This is, of course, only the Explorer's ready-made explanation. A silent smile is the epitome of ambiguity; it may also be understood as a sign of amusement caused by the foreigner's obvious skepticism. It may even be the smile of an expectancy that is sure of its eventual fulfillment.

In view of the fact that Kafka experimented in the fragments with the idea of allowing the executed officer to reappear, this last interpretation would seem plausible. In this case the bystanders are partisans of the old Commandant, as the officer predicted. They form a group quite apart from the officer, who, we learn, is ashamed of the lowliness of this burial place and has made several attempts to exhume the Commandant's remains. As partisans they have gone underground and have buried their master in their midst. One of them may have inscribed this "testament" on the tombstone. Perhaps they even know the exact number of years after which their leader will return. In any case it is the "good message" of the "testament" which unites the meek and oppressed dock laborers into a flock of disciples. There may even be among them fishermen who were forced into their new profession by the new Commandant's reforms. The smiling presence of these disciples changes the teahouse into a cleverly camouflaged sanctuary. In this light it can no longer be viewed as a somewhat exotic counterpart of a European coffeehouse, where rumors are also bred and many divergent sects convene. Its atmosphere is now more unified and assumes the air of a sacred shrine. Following this trend of thought to its conclusion, we may compare the teahouse with another old inn from which another old belief, Judaism, proceeded into the world, rejuvenated, as Christianity. The execution machine may be likened to the Cross, the suicide of the officer to a sacrificial death. The words on the tombstone, "Have faith and wait!" acquire an almost evangelical ring. The imagery of the story as a whole suddenly seems to carry definite overtones of Christian symbolism.

But as soon as we take the inscription on the old Commandant's grave seriously, a strictly religious interpretation of "In the Penal Colony" becomes untenable. The faith that the old Commandant's followers are admonished to preserve cannot be anything but belief in their master's rigorous martial law. This law is no more to be identified with Judaism than Christian hope is to be derived from the old martinet's return to the Colony. The prophecy promises the recapture of the island, and from all the intelligence we have gathered about the old Commandant's attitude we may safely infer that the conquest will be by force. There will be violence, bloodshed, and the blind execution of an inhuman law. So well has Kafka succeeded in identifying the old Commandant with his infernal machine that the reemergence of the one is bound to be followed by the reconstruction of the other. The war of recovery will be fought and won under the sign of the torturing machine. The chances are that many a one who is now hoping for the old Commandant's return will find himself strapped one day to its Bed, the Harrow ready to imprint his offense upon his body.

The prophecy of the teahouse scene reopens the story of "In the Penal Colony" and extends it into an infinite future. The promised return of the old Commandant is intended to hint at a second coming of the execution machine and its deadly writing. The real hero of the story, the "peculiar piece of apparatus," survives in spite of its ruin, unconquered and unconquerable. Kafka did not find an end to the visions of horror which haunted him.

Walter H. Sokel

On "The Country Doctor"

Kafka's work can be called a spiritual autobiography clothed in metaphoric disguise. In a diary entry of August 6, 1914, Kafka noted that his sense for the presentation of his "dreamlike inner life" had stunted all his other interests and talents and had become the only quality that could afford him full satisfaction. Indeed, the oneiric character of Kafka's writings strikes every reader. Their enigmatic suggestiveness is their most pronounced feature. They are like dreams in that they compel interpretation but seem to withhold the key. Sometimes his stories did grow out of dreams, and the dreams Kafka frequently relates in his diaries show a striking resemblance to his stories. Yet his writings differ profoundly from those of the surrealists who jotted down their dreams in automatic writing. Unlike theirs, Kafka's narratives are thoroughly disciplined. They are by no means simple copies of dreams; rather they are structures analogous to dreams in some essential respects.

One of these characteristics is the peculiar relationship of Kafka's narratives to metaphor. His stories tend to present enactments of metaphors buried in language, not only in the German language in which he wrote but also in the universal symbolism of prerational thought. Basic metaphors by which prescientific language expresses experiences, attitudes, and relationships become event in Kafka's tales. He reinstates, or re-creates, the pictorial expressiveness which the original metaphor, frozen in a cliché or idiom, once conveyed. Thus Kafka's writing conforms to or repeats the activity of the dreaming mind. As Freud has shown in his *Interpretation of Dreams,* a work with which Kafka was familiar, dreams speak in the pictorial language speech once

Reprinted from Walter H. Sokel, Franz Kafka *(1966), by permission of Columbia University Press.*

was. They take the metaphors hidden in speech literally and act them out as visualized events.

A few examples might help to clarify the preceding remarks. A decisive and profound experience is said to "leave a mark"; a lasting memory is "engraved" on one. Kafka's *The Penal Colony* depicts both metaphors as physical happenings. The penal machine slowly kills the condemned prisoner by literally engraving (German: *einkerben*) on his flesh the law he transgressed. He dies, in fact, of his remembering this lesson; "the mark left" by the law kills him. German usage applies the term *Ungeziefer* (vermin) to persons considered low and contemptible, even as our usage of "cockroach" describes a person deemed a spineless and miserable character. The traveling salesman Gregor Samsa, in Kafka's "The Metamorphosis," is "like a cockroach" because of his spineless and abject behavior and parasitic wishes. However, Kafka drops the world "like" and has the metaphor become reality when Gregor Samsa wakes up finding himself turned into a giant vermin. With this metamorphosis, Kafka reverses the original act of metamorphosis carried out by thought when it forms metaphor; for metaphor is always "metamorphosis." Kafka transforms metaphor back into his fictional reality, and this counter-metamorphosis becomes the starting point of his tale. German usage calls a sexually indecent and obscene character a "pig" or "swine" *(Schwein)*. In Kafka's tale, "A Country Doctor," the groom who assaults the doctor's maid walks out of the doctor's pigsty.

Kafka's narratives do not stop with reactivating single metaphors. They connect organically the enactment of one metaphor with the enactments of others; together these establish a narrative development. "A Country Doctor" will serve as an example.

The swinish groom stands in a fateful relation to the protagonist of the story, the country doctor, through whose consciousness alone we witness the events. The doctor had lived next to his maid, Rose, without noticing her as a woman. As soon as she presents herself to him as desirable, the groom steps out of the doctor's unused[1] pigsty and seeks to rape her. The unused pigsty belongs to the doctor; it is, in the words of the story, "his own." The groom is, then, literally a dweller of the doctor's forgotten lower depths. He embodies the doctor's unused sex drive in a strikingly literal way. The doctor's consciousness does not acknowledge his responsibility for the event he himself has called forth when he kicked the door of the pigsty open "absent-mindedly" and thus released the groom. The sudden emergence of the "filthy" contents

[1] The original text uses the German word for "unused"—*unbenützt*—which the English translation renders as "uninhabited."

of the doctor's depths—the unacknowledged component of his self—now overpowers his humanity and makes the girl a prey of bestial desire. In Kafka's stories, acts and omissions reveal what consciousness hides from itself. Not consciousness—the explicit comments of the story—but the narrated events show the true meaning of Kafka's tale. "A Country Doctor" begins with a call of the night bell summoning the doctor to a patient. However, his horse had died from overexertion and he cannot follow his call. In his dilemma, he calls "absent-mindedly"[2] (that is, unconsciously) on his forgotten pigsty, releasing the swinish groom and a team of "unearthly horses" and allows the groom to take the girl. Contrary to his verbal protestations, the doctor does in fact leave Rose behind with the groom. She is the price for the groom's aid.

Images and plot of this tale enable us to see Kafka's works as pieces of an autobiography in metaphoric disguise. The "call" of the night bell is a translation into sensory terms of Kafka's "call" to literature, which he understood as an art of healing and self-preservation, a "doctor's" art. Writing for Kafka was night work in two respects: literally, because he had no time for it during the day; figuratively, because he had to delve into the nocturnal regions of his mind, the representation of which he called his fatal talent. The death of the horse shows that no normal and natural way is available for transporting the self to its calling. As the doctor finds his self in absent-mindedness, Kafka notes that he had done his best writing when all rational control was lifted. In one night, with "an outpouring of his soul," he wrote "The Judgment," which remained his favorite work and model of all others.

"A Country Doctor" presents in the hieroglyphic language of dreams a clear and exact presentation of Kafka's inspirational process and the problems it posed for his life. In a revealing letter to Max Brod, in 1922, he calls his writing a "descent to the dark powers, an unchaining of spirits whose natural state it is to be bound servants." The description fits the groom of "A Country Doctor," who, instead of serving the self, expels it and takes over its vacated house. In that same letter to Brod, Kafka says that, in order to devote himself to literature, the writer must sacrifice fulfillment in life. The "unearthly horses" of inspiration, called forth from the unsavory depths, transport the doctor away from life, woman, and home. He is shown literally "carried away," "in the transport" of inspiration, since his unearthly team of horses proceeds without his conscious will and carries him off instantaneously and miraculously to his vocational destination. This destination is an existen-

---

[2] The original text uses the German word for "absent-mindedly"—*zerstreut*—which the English translation renders as "confused."

tial encounter, symbolized by his being undressed and put in the same bed with his sick childhood self, the boy patient to whom he has been called.

The two houses pictorialize the two poles of the doctor's existence. In his own house, the house of the self, the doctor abandoned the possibility of erotic fulfillment; in the other house, the house of the patient, he is to dedicate himself to his art, which is the confrontation with the congenital wound of mortality. The hero's ambivalence is such that he cannot be content at either pole. At home he sacrifices the girl to his mission; but at his destination he regrets the price he has paid and wants to return. His split existence, his inability to choose, becomes pure image in the doctor's final condition. He is shown riding aimlessly between the houses; the distance between them has become infinite, and he cannot stay at either place.

"A Country Doctor" became the title story of a volume of Kafka's short pieces published in 1919 and dedicated to his father, which makes the importance Kafka attached to this particular work quite evident. The detailed examination of its plot and images has enabled us to understand the allegorical principle informing Kafka's writings. His images are pictorial translations of over-riding personal concerns in which personal meaning acquires universal significance.

Any individual work by Kafka may baffle the reader when considered in isolation. If examined within the context of Kafka's other works and personal documents, the nature and meaning of his images become clear. The individual work will then appear as a variation of a single theme—the inner autobiography of the author—and a step in its development. Each work is aesthetically self-sufficient and, if completed and published by Kafka himself, a complete and satisfying statement of one approach to the master theme.

Hermann J. Weigand

Franz Kafka's "The Burrow" ("Der Bau"): An Analytical Essay

Every reader of "The Burrow" who is even moderately familiar with Kafka's life and work cannot fail to be struck by the realization that there is an intimate relation, often amounting to identity, between the author and the persona of his story.[1] A symbolical interpretation is fully warranted and has often been undertaken, with varying success. It is not my purpose, however, to take such an approach in this essay. I have been intent on analyzing the story in terms of its own data. The reader will be well rewarded by supplementing this account with a study of many others, including those listed in brief notes.

"I have made the burrow habitable, and I think it has shaped up well."[2] This, the first sentence of what is probably Kafka's last story, prompts us to examine the blueprint of the structure in question.

Having taken precautions against flooding from the outset, the speaker has built in a dry, sandy spot, deep underground, a central stronghold, spacious, smooth, and elegantly vaulted, large enough to accomodate provisions to last him for half a year without crowding. From this stronghold ten tunnels radiate, rising, dipping, curving to conform to functional needs and to features of the terrain. At intervals of one hundred meters, each of the tunnels expands to a platform suitable for

---

[1] This essay is based on Franz Kafka's "Der Bau" as contained in *Gesammelte Schriften*, ed. Max Brod (New York: Schocken Books, 1946), v, 172-214. The English renditons are mine.

[2] Ich habe den Bau eingerichtet und er scheint wohlgelungen (p. 172).

Reprinted by permission of the Modern Language Association of America from PMLA, *Vol. 87, No. 2 (March 1972).*

rest or storage. There are more than fifty of these platforms, each of them individually designed and distinguishable by feel and sight. The tunnels are again crisscrossed by a network of connecting galleries or corridors. One of these has the function of communicating with the world aboveground. Before leading to a vent, thinly covered by a layer of moss, it expands into a maze of intricate design, a feature intended to baffle and impede any potential prowler who might have stumbled upon the well-concealed vent. This underground habitat, serving the material needs of security, shelter, and sustenance, a self-contained world as it were, is beautifully air-conditioned, thanks to the channels dug by the wood mice and other small fry. The master-builder prides himself on having incorporated these small animals into his plans, not only for regulating the ventilation but also letting them serve as an unfailing if modest food supply. While there is no reason to doubt the truth of the account as respects all other features of the burrow, we detect a note of swagger in his reference to the ventilation: he is claiming credit for a feature that resulted as an automatic by-product of any burrower's layout.

The underground structure, planned on so vast a scale and requiring years of unremitting effort to execute—can it have been undertaken merely to provide for the material needs of security, shelter, and sustenance? Of course not. Every page of the account tells us rather that it was designed to answer its creator's craving for self-glorification.

For our story to cohere, we have to venture into the realm of unreality. What kind of creature is the builder of this burrow? Generically speaking, he is a hybrid of man and animal, a large, furry, tailless carnivore with a powerful dome of a forehead that constitutes his chief tool. His wants and needs are strictly those of an animal. However, his powers of abstract reasoning and introspection and the sensitive differentiation of his emotional life are on a high human level. He is an artist-engineer, skilled in discussing the problems of his craft, with a passion for meticulous and often irritatingly pedantic exactness. This master-builder has no supernatural endowment, no innate knowledge. He is totally devoid of curiosity or imagination concerning anything except himself and his burrow. In his capacity of both man and animal, the master-builder is a loner. Without clan, family, or overt sex life, he is asocial and antisocial. Engrossed entirely in his own problems, he has no rapport with any possible audience. Society as complement and self-fulfillment is replaced by the burrow, the product of his brain and muscle. The burrow comes to assume the status of the self objectified, bearing the same relation to its designer as body and soul in ordinary parlance. The master-builder and his burrow are one.

What about the living social world outside the burrow? Has it ceased to exist for him? Not at all. Its presence on the other side constantly makes itself felt. It is perhaps never wholly absent from his consciousness, but it exists only as a foil, generating a state of tension within him. It turns out that this state of tension is as necessary to his well-being as the fulfillment of his desire for isolation and security.

Not being a synthetic creature, although a loner, our master-builder must have sprung from a social background. We probe the texture of his self-revelation for every hint of its specific character and we scan the record with eagerness for some clue to the mystery of his withdrawal from society. Although we shall never get beyond very general surmises, let us see what we can learn of his social background, both human and animal.

To begin with the human side, at an early point of the account he speaks of legends regarding mysterious, inconceivably powerful creatures that dwell in the interior of the earth; their powers render null any attempt to arrive at absolute security. He must be the beneficiary of a tradition in this respect. The same applies to a later reference to a Providence as a feature of religious instruction. As for his technical education, he makes his calculations in terms of the metric system. If I speak of his design as a blueprint, this would seem to be justified in its literal meaning. And there is a hint of his familiarity with delicate machinery when he remarks on the enormous acuity of his hearing. At a late point of his account, a remark slips out of his mouth to the effect that he now works like a laborer, going through the motions of the act under the eye of a foreman, thus betraying some familiarity with human labor conditions. Earlier, upon the return to his burrow after a prolonged sojourn and exile aboveground, he greets his tunnels and chats with them "as with friends," then checks himself because the ring of the word "friend" awakens emotions he is determined to suppress. Twice we come across a turn of speech that seems to reflect a background of literary education. "There in the dark moss is the spot where I could be destroyed."[3] To a German ear this sounds like a quotation from Schiller's *Don Carlos*. The second passage of this sort, expressing his confidence that he is not destined or doomed to spend the remainder of his life in the open, away from his burrow, reads, "Someone will call me to him and I shall not be able to resist his invitation."[4] The somewhat ironic humor of this context tends to disguise the fact that this sounds like a reminiscence of the sinister role of the commendatore in Mozart's *Don Giovanni*. But I

---

[3] . . . dort an jener Stelle im dunklen Moos bin ich sterblich . . . (p. 172). Cf. Schiller's *Don Carlos:* Hier ist die Stelle, wo ich sterblich bin (I.vi.865).

[4] . . . dass mich . . . jemand zu sich rufen wird, dessen Einladung ich nicht werde widerstehen können (p. 183).

would not labor the meaning of these passages because their quotational quality seems to attach to Kafka rather than to his hero. This exhausts the list of reminiscences that tend to shed light on the hero's background conceived in human terms.

On the animal level, basking in the first flush of pride at the achievement of his master burrow, his memory ranges back with mock sympathy to contemplate the packs of forest roamers dependent on improvised shelter and subject to the vicissitudes of chance. At some time or other he must have shared in this life of vagabondage. Much later, while outside the burrow, tormented by inhibitions and hoping against hope to overcome the frustration that bars him from returning home, his rage at the thought of one of his own kind, a connoisseur of building but a marauder, snooping about his burrow and threatening to dispossess him, arouses him to an orgiastic pitch of lust and fury. I cannot help wondering whether this murderous fantasy is not the reactivation of some hostile encounter with one of his fellows, an outrage perpetrated against himself. Was it this, perhaps, coupled with a humiliation too painful to avow to himself, that made him decide to go it alone for the rest of his life?

Before turning to an analysis of the content, we must come to grips with the formal pattern of the discourse. We first meet the speaker at the prime of his life, after he has just completed the object of his ambition. We hear his voice, coming, as we subsequently learn, from the interior of the burrow. He engages in a progressive recital, not meant as a communication because all social contacts have ceased to exist for him.[5] Nevertheless, in its character of human speech, it comes through to us as a communication. From the moment of his first utterance, the recital has the character of an emerging present, continuous with the flow of his life. There is no narrative element in the strict sense of the word. Only as occasional reminiscences, dating back beyond the achievement of his building project, the preterite tense, hallmark of narration, is used.[6] The flow of his recital, a matter of ninety minutes, is synchronous with the flow of his life, condensing a span of experience that extends over many years. His speech flows forward as his life flows forward, encountering unforeseen troubles of a psychological nature. It flows on as he finds himself beset by restlessness and anxiety, inhibi-

---

[5] There is one exception. On the first page he defends himself against the imputation of cowardice. This presupposes his having a mental *Gegenüber* in mind. But this aspect is dropped, never to be taken up again.

[6] An exception to this occurs on p. 184, when he sums up the experiences of the first week spent aboveground after leaving the burrow.

tions, phobias, and all the symptoms that add up to a state of psychoneurosis. It flows on, recording its progression from virility to advanced age; it flows on, the speaker's strength of mind giving way to senile dementia and exhaustion. Some patterns of life tend to repeat themselves and words like "occasionally," "sometimes," "now and then," (*"öfters," "manchmal," "zu Zeiten"*) have to be employed, but these are always followed by an iterative or durative present. The ninety-minute recital and the life span of many years run on two parallel but qualitatively different rails, beginning and ending, mirabile dictu, at the same point of time. This is one way of equating enacted time with imagined time. The monologue is strictly grammatical, a discourse composed of precisely organized, often infinitely complicated sentences, never interrupted by those abrupt and fragmentary musings that carry the flavor of what we term interior monologue. This is altogether different from stream of consciousness thinking, which abounds in broken off phrases, unfinished sentences, incoherent terms, and helter-skelter associations. In this recital there is not a sentence that fails to reach the objective of its grammatical aim.[7] This sense of our participating in an unbroken time continuum is all the more remarkable because the greater part of its forty-two pages is devoted not to events and actions, but rather to speculations, problems, working hypotheses put forward, modified, rejected, reversed, and taken up afresh. There is a zigzag motion of ratiocination based on premises that look sound enough but shift like quicksand. For the attentive listener, all this verbalizing is full of ominous overtones to whose wavelength the speaker's ear is not attuned. And the deeper, often tragic meaning of its formulation never seems to rise to the threshold of his consciousness.

Let us try to envisage this piece of Kafka's prose in terms of its structural articulation. Several avenues to this end suggest themselves. One of the easiest lines to follow is to see the story in terms of the

---

[7] Most critics are completely silent about the form of the recital. These include Wilhelm Emrich, "Der Bau und das Selbst des Menschen," in *Franz Kafka* (Bonn: Athenäum, 1958), pp. 172-86; Walter F. Sokel, "Das Schweigen des Baus," in *Franz Kafka: Tragik und Ironie* (München: A. Langen-G. Müller, 1964), pp. 371-87; Heinrich Henel, "Kafka's 'Der Bau,' or How to Escape from a Maze," in *The Discontinuous Tradition: Studies in German Literature in Honour of Ernest Ludwig Stahl* (Oxford: Oxford Univ. Press, 1970), pp. 224-46; Heinz Politzer, *Franz Kafka: Parable and Paradox* (Ithaca, N. Y.: Cornell Univ. Press, 1962), in his chapter "The Castle Within" (pp. 318-33) has a lapse of memory in speaking of the story as told by an old master-builder. To my knowledge, the only study including a precise description of Kafka's narrative technique in "The Burrow," but limited to technical matters exclusively, is to be found in Hartmut Binder's brief chapter, "Der Bau," in *Motiv und Gestaltung bei Franz Kafka* (Bonn: H. Bouvier, 1966), pp. 340-46.

changes of locale. This approach would yield five major divisions: (1) The speaker is inside his burrow at the outset and he continues to speak from inside it for about one quarter of the whole. (2) The speaker has emerged into the open for a relatively brief change of air as he thinks, but this excursion takes on the character of a period of exile lasting for weeks, at the very least. All this time he is subject to extreme mental agitation. He wants to go home but insurmountable inhibitions bar his return. This, for me the most striking and imaginatively executed part of Kafka's story, also accounts for about one quarter of the whole. (3) Back in the burrow once more, the stillness of which he has praised as its most beautiful feature, he finds himself disturbed by faint, intermittent sounds suggestive of hissing or whistling. These torment him in ever increasing measure. This part of the story, constituting the longest section, deals with his attempts to define the sound, to locate its point of origin, to speculate upon its possible causes and on possible means of eliminating them, in the course of which he becomes worn down and enfeebled. This process of progressive attrition is measured in terms of years. (4) When mental torture and enfeeblement have reached a certain point, he yields to an automatic urge to escape. Having threaded his way through the maze, he settles down at the bottom of the vent that leads into the open. Here, at last, the tormenting sounds of the interior no longer haunt him. He finds a degree of relief, and in continuing to brood over his problem, his memory comes upon a remarkable incident that occupied his mind while he was at work on the maze. Having correlated that incident with the torturing images that presently haunt him, he feels an irresistible urge to return to the locale of his woes, wishing at the same time that his enfeeblement were too great to permit it. This fourth part is rather short. (5) He resumes his restless wanderings through his passageways and finally settles down in the stronghold to speculate on the principles of an efficacious defense and on the chances of negotiating with a potential intruder. Beset by futile speculations, he concludes, the only practical course to pursue is to consume as great a portion of his provisions as his strength still permits. This, the last part, is also short. Summing these up by captions, we have (1) inside the burrow, (2) in exile above the ground, (3) back in the burrow, (4) down in the vent between two worlds, (5) once more in the burrow.

Another approach to the structure would see the story in two parts, the first being not much more than a takeoff point, showing the speaker in his prime, and at the height of his achievement, presenting some fairly precise personality traits and letting us glimpse the disposition of the adolescent at the time the great project got under way. Beyond that point no early memories are overtly acknowledged. Part two would then comprise all the rest of the story. It would be a story of a progressive mental illness, of creeping nervous tension and anxiety, of inner conflict and tribulation, leading by way of various crises to eventual senility and collapse. This would be the clinical view. It might be reduced, perhaps too simply, to the formula: having spent his adolescence and the early years of his manhood in the execution of a grandiose idea, the designer, artist, and engineer in one still has a great surplus of mental and animal energy, but he does not know what to do with it. His simple wants—security, shelter, sustenance—are more than adequately provided for and the great structure is a tangible symbol of his sense of self-glorification. Now his excess mental and physical energy, finding no rewarding outlet, in the total absence of any social life, turns sour. The stages in the decline of his mental health, corresponding to stages of the aging process, might warrant the following labels: (1) creeping neurosis, (2) aboulia (paralysis of the will) in exile, (3) a psychosis, a haunting hallucination, (4) religion, (5) senile dementia and total enfeeblement of animal energy. I trust that these labels will become meaningful in the course of our analysis. I see the most important qualitative escalation of of his mental illness in the emergence of the hallucination—the hissing and whistling noise.

Another approach would stress a structural dichotomy in terms of the great *Umschlag,* the total turnabout of the inner center of gravity which takes place during his exile. From being the beneficiary of the burrow's protection, he reverses the roles to fancy himself its guardian. This attitude, developed in great detail, carries over into the later phase of psychotic hallucination, with great imaginative intensity. All the foregoing approaches are proper and should be turned to as mutually complementary in analyzing the story.

The opening paragraph furnishes an abundance of leads from which to form a precise image of the personality traits and temperament of the hero-antihero. With the hindsight afforded by knowing the whole course of the story, a skilled psychiatrist should, in fact, be able to predict the terminal stage on the basis of the introductory statements. He would soon detect the almost imperceptible curve of a large, systematically inward-turning mental spiral that must eventually end up in a point. In introducing his burrow, the speaker intones a note of serene satisfaction. His voice is calm and precise, his account of the problems he encountered is meticulously lucid; he speaks with the air of one in command who deserves unqualified credence. Ends and means have been brought into focus, everything has been achieved in accordance with precise calculations, it is a triumph of the reasoning mind over a challenging environment. With the knowledge of innumerable potential enemies to endanger his life, he has steered a course of firm caution, the rational counterpart of fear. Caution tells him that absolute security can never be achieved in this world. By way of legends he has learned that there are sinister, irrational forces within the earth too powerful for any individual to cope with; they can annihilate without a trace of warning. (We might think of earthquakes, by way of example.) Caution requires such knowledge, but it must never be allowed to intrude into rational calculations.

The first material detail to catch our eye is a hole that leads nowhere. After countless false starts in the vicinity, all of them carefully obliterated, this hole has been left at a distance of a thousand paces from the point where he began to establish his burrow. Why did he leave that hole for some potential enemy to pry into? From the very outset there is an ambivalence about his motives. By leaving this hole, the hero exhibits a dash of recklessness, an overweening sense of security, an air of bravado. Repudiating the insinuation of cowardice,[8] he wants to be thought of as bold (*kühn*). The hole is left to potential enemies as a lure and a decoy. Someone coming upon it unaware is intended to surmise that something worthwhile is waiting for a discoverer's ingenuity; at the same time there is only a minimal possibility of his ever finding it. By this device our hero has staked out the position of a game of hide-and-seek. There are innumerable potential players, but no second player ever materializes to lead him a chase or make him face up to a confrontation. To make his life worth living, the excitement of danger seems as necessary as the need for security. Since his subsequent experience never converts the potential threat to a real threat, his imagination will be called on to supply the deficiency. Fear of a confrontation neatly balances his wish to be discovered. This ambivalence is the field of force in which the whole story has its being. Intuitively aware of this, he delights in aphorisms to give it polished expression: " . . . some acts of cunning are so subtle as to work their own destruction."[9] At this point he knows the concept of tragic irony without feeling the shudder of his own tragic involvement. Another aphorism: "As is so often the case, the very stance of caution requires the risk of life."[10] Another: ". . . and the pleasure which an ingenious brain takes in its own operations is sometimes the only reason for continuing on one's calculations."[11]

The very design of his structure reveals the same basic ambivalence

---

[8] Cf. n. 4.

[9] . . . mance List ist so fein, dass sie sich selbst umbringt . . . (p. 172).

[10] . . . gerade die Vorsicht verlangt, wie leider so oft, das Risiko des Lebens (p. 173).

[11] . . . und die Freude des scharfsinnigen Kopfes an sich selbst ist manchmal die alleinige Ursache dessen, dass man weiterrechnet (p. 173).

of purpose. It is all so well coordinated, with its tunnels radiating from the central stronghold, as to seem an exemplary instance of the principle, form follows function. Yet the vastness of its design makes it disproportionate to his simple animal needs. To be sure, the scale of the blueprint makes its execution a symbol of the designer's demand for self-glorification, but this caters to the wants of the brain, not those of the animal. He tells us repeatedly of his dislike for hard physical labor, and on this score he concedes his construction to have proved disproportionately costly. We think of the thousands of hammer blows delivered by his forehead to firm up the vault of his stronghold, with the ooze of his own lifeblood serving as the binder.[12] The idea of function is self-defeating in another respect: the number of his tunnels and that of the channels crisscrossing them is so great as to increase by very large odds the danger of a potential enemy stumbling by accident upon the burrow in the course of its own digging. Such an accident would get the game of hide-and-seek agoing.

There is ambivalence, of course, in staking everything upon maximum security while realizing that total security is impossible. Thus, at an early point, his allusion to legends prompts him to admit that the exit, though his only hope, is more likely than not to work his ruin. I think this marks the first strong indication of a pessimistic foreboding. Ambivalence is found again in the statements concerning his life within the burrow. The most delectable thing about the burrow is its stillness, radiating an atmosphere of peace, but it is deceptive and can be broken at any moment. And there is his admission in the opening paragraph that life within the burrow rarely affords a really quiet hour. If we take this as referring to the struggle for survival which goes on unabating as long as there is life, we now find his sense of uneasiness taking on very specific forms. He has dreams, worries, anxieties, nightmares, his sleep is fitful, and he is apt to wake up with a violent start. "Aufschrecken" is a word repeatedly used to describe it. Ever since "moving in" he has busied himself with relocating his provisions with a view to greater security, trying now this, now that, performing a vast amount of back-breaking work, sometimes in a nightmarish state of panic, all to no purpose, as he finds after restoring his supplies at last to their original locale. It is to the credit of his personality, to be sure, that his temperament forbids his vegetating in the peaceful possession of a house like any

---

[12] Sokel puts the main emphasis on charging the hero with narcissism and self-indulgence. To my way of thinking he vastly overstresses the hero's indulgence in a sense of ease. I think of him as driven and on the go practically all the time. As to his protestation that he has always taken off too much time, instead of working, I regard these self-reproaches as morbid.

bourgeois grown fat, but this does not alter the fact that he is by this time a very sick animal. Ruefully and irrationally he tells himself that his blueprint should have made provision for a number of strongholds (although we cannot for the life of us see how this would have increased his security). He realized this need dimly while at work on the structure, but then it was too late to fit this enlargement into his plan, and in any case it would have required an amount of physical energy beyond his capacity. So he finds that his blueprint has an irremediable flaw and he contents himself with the aphoristic reflection: "There is bound to be a flaw in everything of which there is but a single model."[13]

This admission is a formulation of what we may call existential guilt as a shortcoming implicit in the conditions of life itself. It is reinforced by a more specific, passive guilt, a refusal to implement maturing insight with corresponding practical improvements in detail, as in his criticism of the maze. This sense of guilt continues to haunt him. Without doubt he also feels an active sense of guilt in the wake of those rare gluttonous orgies which, leaving him in a state unfit for defense, seem rather like a symptom of nervous exhaustion than an ingrained vice.[14] In a later stage, when he speaks of himself as suffering punishment for guilt that he is not aware of, all the above factors must have coalesced into a vague feeling which his logical analysis cannot fathom.

The most startling sentence to have reached our ears up to this point comes as part of his speculation for the need of several strongholds. As a rule, one does not suffice; however, he hopes that in his case one will suffice "by way of exception, by way of grace, probably because Providence has a special stake in the preservation of my forehead, the stamping-hammer."[15] It is surprising as such to realize that he should have a concept of a Providence, but we cannot undertake to interpret its application to his case at this particular point with any assurance of being right. It is phrased in the low key of a rational proposition that is accepted as probable. Only the word "gnadenweise" rises above the level of the phrasing to express an attitude of faith. He is favored, but if Providence has a stake in the preservation of his forehead, the relation is a reciprocal matter of interdependence. Is it possible that he could have kept under cover a layer of mystical feeling akin to the epigram of Angelus Silesius?

[13] . . . wie überhaupt dort immer ein Fehler ist, wo man von irgend erwas nur ein Exemplar besitzt (p. 178). Politzer persuasively argues that words like *Exemplar* and *Erstlingswerk* carry overtones of literary activity, rendering plausibility to his interpretation of "The Burrow" as a symbol of Kafka's literary work.

[14] Sokel to the contrary.

[15] . . . ausnahmsweise, gnadenweise, wahrscheinlich, weil der Vorsehung an der Erhaltung meiner Stirn besonders gelegen ist, des Stampfhammers, . . . (p. 178).

Ich weiss, dass ohne mich Gott nicht ein Nu kann leben,
Werd' ich zunicht, er muss sofort den Geist aufgeben.

I know that without me, God cannot live for a moment.
If I am annihilated, he must at once give up the ghost.

If Providence has its eye upon him, he must be instrumental in the working out of a higher design. Perhaps the reference to Providence is only a belated echo, possibly a bitterly cynical echo, of a great wave of optimism that animated him during his adolescence. Does not many a young man of genius instinctively feel himself to be a darling of the gods—witness Goethe, in whom the feeling was very strong, more than traces of it persisting into his old age—and was our builder not a genius, the designer of a structure that deserved the admiration owing to a priceless work of art! I confess my inability to fathom the emotional overtones that accompany this statement. Unless everything deceives me, the existence of a Providence and the existence of himself as being assigned a special role in the pursuance of its purposes are stated as matters of fact, whereas the aspect of probability applies only to the present means, sufficing in his own particular case by way of exception and by way of grace.

Reduced by humiliating reflections, by senseless physical toil, by the alternation of compulsive fasts and orgies, and driven by a persecution complex only dimly avowed at this point, he looks for a change of environment to restore his mental balance. According to his phrasing, to absent himself for long would seem "too severe a punishment." This curious statement becomes clear only in the light of his admission, when out in the open, that he was seriously troubled at the time: "And I find, strangely enough, that I am not in as bad shape as I often believed to be the case and as I shall probably again believe when I descend into my house."[16]

He has been in the habit of leaving his burrow from time to time to engage in the hunt and replenish his supplies, and for all we are told, everything went well. But now he has got himself into a state which opposes great obstacles to such a maneuver. For the first time we hear of the maze, located this side of the hole of ascent, on the construction of which he lavished all the enthusiasm of his youth and which he has now come to look upon with a mixture of condescension, admiration, and fears regarding its solidity. Forgetting all his brave talk of a rational pur-

---

[16] Und ich finde, dass es merkwürdigerweise nicht so schlimm mit mir steht, wie ich oft glaubte und wie ich wahrscheinlich wieder glauben werde, wenn ich in mein Haus hinabsteige (p. 183).

suance of well-calculated ends, his speech shifts to the exposure of feelings with which he cannot cope. The maze has become a symbol of something to be dreaded. He deliberately avoids it on his daily walks. He tries to suppress his awareness of its existence. It has become a terror zone, the mere approach to which makes him feel skinned alive. Why this should be so we do not clearly understand, because all the reasons he advances to explain his dread are prima facie rationalizations, suppressing something that lies beyond. Is it that he is tormented by an unconscious tension between his underground habitation and the world above? Is it that he feels himself a captive of his burrow, yet so acclimatized to its walls that he dreads the prospect of the unfamiliar? Is it that he fears that once having escaped, he will never have the courage to return, thereby forfeiting all that his life has stood for? He expatiates on the distress in a way to create the impression that he has been a prey to these neurotic torments on previous occasions when he felt the urge to have a change of air. To this purpose he makes free use of expressions like "sometimes," "occasionally," "at times." In shifting from these iteratives to "today" *(heute)*[17] and successfully taking us with him over the hurdle and up over the "trapdoor" *(Falltür)*[18] he is ignorant of the dimensions of the neurosis awaiting him on the other side. He—and the reader as well—is ignorant of the fact that this self-imposed period of exile is destined to mark his last communication with the world outside.

Not all his dread of entering the maze was a matter of rationalization. He was clearly aware that it was of too flimsy a construction to withstand a determined attack, but contenting himself with this insight he has stubbornly refused to undertake the work of rebuilding it, thus incurring the guilt of negligence. Of course, as usual, he stifles the inner voice of self-reproach by the reflection that it is now too late to undertake so extensive a change—he could not escape observation if he were to do so now. Moreover, he compensates by a recurrent wish-fulfillment dream, that he has succeeded in making the maze impregnable *(uneinnehmbar)*. The tears of joy that stream down his whiskers on awakening from this dream are sweeter evidently than the drops of sweat that would have been the by-product of actual labor.

The moment of decision, of actually lifting the moss cover and slipping out, is built up as a dramatic episode. The suspense takes the form of a series of questions addressed to himself in which reluctance is balanced by a desire to escape. Even the impulse to leave everything behind for good is entertained for a moment, only to be repudiated later.

[17] This is the only instance of *heute* occurring in the sense of "today," in contrast to other passages where it has the meaning of "nowadays."

[18] Politzer, relying on a faulty recollection, speaks of "trapdoors" and "fortifications."

Once he is outside, the web of anxieties is dissipated for a moment. He feels a resurgence of vital energies. His voice has the old ring of mastery. The concern for the hunt is the first thing to engage his attention. The strenuous life agrees with him. Everything considered, spartan fare outside is better than luxury at home. It is great to be roughing it, because this is a vacation freely chosen and to be terminated whenever he tires of the game. This is where he says, "Someone will call me to him and I shall not be able to resist the invitation." For him this phrasing expresses an exuberance of animal spirits at variance with the ominous overtones that strike our ears. This is the first time that he personifies his burrow by referring to it as "someone" *(jemand)*. Here he does so playfully, without realizing what a deeply obsessive fixation this personalization is destined to become.

The joy of being on his own, away from the burrow, is short-lived. He soon yields to an impulse to return to its vicinity and lie in wait, keeping his eye fixed on the entrance. Up to the point of his exile, he had persuaded himself that he had built the great structure primarily as a means for his protection, but now that he is on the other side, the roles become curiously reversed. His inner compass wings around by 180 degrees: it is the burrow which must now be protected at all costs, and the role of protector has devolved on him. What was designed to be the instrument of his protection has become the object of his solicitude. He and his burrow are now like two poles of an elliptical field of force.

At once his morbid anxiety returns. He has already spent a week with his eye trained on the trapdoor. If we are to believe him, there is a great deal of traffic passing through the area, much of it potentially hostile, but no chance passerby has evinced any curiosity to investigate the spot. He keeps on the watch, prepared for a ferocious defense, alternating with impulses toward flight. As the time continues to pass without any untoward incident, he ruminates on the possibility that the world's hostility toward him may have abated, or that his structure radiates a mysterious power exempting him from the universal struggle for survival. (This is the second time that he manifests an attitude of mystical faith.) We see in this how the personalization of the structure has taken root in its builder. He develops what he calls a childish fantasy to the effect that he might find his greatest happiness in being on the watch forever and ever, guarding his house against attack and imagining himself as cradled inside it.[19] From such daydreams he starts up in sudden terror, finding himself deluged by new anxieties regarding the tenuous security afforded by the burrow when he is inside it. There comes a time

---

[19] Emrich ably develops the metaphysical implications of the hero's ruminative introspection, but in doing so he ignores many other features of great importance.

when he leaves his place of observation, tired of life in the open, persuaded that there is nothing more to be learned here, either now or later. "And I am inclined to take leave of everything here, to descend into the burrow and never to return." His choice of phrasing in the passage quoted surely reveals an unconscious death wish. However, this yearning for return needs but to be expressed for the shuttle of his mind to dart in the opposite direction and cancel out his impulse. The web of reasons to motivate his reluctance is too tangled for us to understand—at least for the present: the act of descending would be designed to focus attention upon him, "a procedure nothing short of spectacular," a thought he finds eminently painful (*sehr quälend*). This would be, he tells us, because he would not know who is watching as he descends and replaces the trapdoor.

But why should this be so painful? He admits to having been spoiled *(verwöhnt)* by having been so long an observer of everything that transpired aboveground. But has he remarked on anything to interest him while lying guard? Has anyone taken the slightest notice of *his* presence? For all the attention paid to him, he might have been wearing a *Tarnkappe*, a cloak of invisibility, in the stream of traffic. We can say, to be sure, equating the creature's position with Kafka's own: in the context of the unconscious death wish, he would find dying very painful and the funeral arrangements would be designed to call attention to one who had long gone unnoticed. Such an interpretation would make sense when applied to the author during the last stage of his long illness, when he was writing this story, but it does not carry the ring of conviction in the context before us. In contrast to many other passages which expose the fallacy of the speaker's reasoning at a glance, the present train of thought, so heavily saturated with emotion, remains obscure in its bearing: ". . . behind my back and after that, behind the readjusted trapdoor." In line with this personal interpretation, the enigmatic remark that follows would be read as Kafka's speculation on the possibility of an afterlife. "It will be made manifest, but no longer to me, or possibly to me also, but too late."

The next stages of his sojourn aboveground can be quickly summarized. As a preliminary to his own descent he stuffs the collected booty down the entrance hole. Finding himself psychologically unable to follow, he constructs a very short observation trench and as time passes, days and weeks going by at the very least, the urge to return home becomes more insistent. During this long spell of inactivity, he is seriously beset by the temptation to abandon his burrow for good and resume a life of roaming in the open. At no time does any sentimental attachment to nature appear as an element of this wish; neither is there any hint throughout the whole account of any thought of returning to society. The diffused dangers to be encountered in such a life everywhere seem preferable to the specific danger which his entrance hole presents. Dismissing this as nonsense, he tries to force a showdown. By running at top speed in broad daylight, he plans to make a dive for his hole, but unnerved, he overshoots it and flings himself into a thicket of briars. Self-inflicted pain, as punishment for what? he muses. But on further thought he justifies his avoidance of the hole by the reflection "that it is really impossible to descend without exposing the most precious thing I have, at least for a little while, to the full view of all those around me, on the ground, in the trees, in the air." "The most precious thing I have . . ." (*das Teuerste, was ich habe* . . .)—this phrase, charged with a high emotional content, is it not a strange designation for a hole stuffed with booty? Yet to relate the phrase to the whole system of underground construction sounds even more improbable because the burrow represents the sum total of what he cherishes, not the most precious part of it. *Preisgeben* is an ambiguous word. It can mean either "abandon" or "expose to view." In this context the latter meaning makes better sense, in fact the only sense. To expose to view the most precious thing he has for even a little while to everything on the ground, in the trees, in the atmosphere—can he have something else in mind? He must have something else in mind, that something which he referred to as making the act of his descent nothing short of spectacular.

If I may be personal for a moment, I remember, after weeks of preoccupation with this story, the exact day and hour on which it struck me in a flash: this passage, and the passage above, as well as a number of passages to follow, must have a sexual meaning, fastidiously concealed because intolerably humiliating the creature's puritanical code. The fear of indecent exposure, and exhibitionism as its counterpart, beset him as manifestations of a libido that torments him. They add an emphatic note of sexual anxiety to those other sources of guilt which we have designated as existential, positive (active), and passive (negative). To imagine his hinder parts exposed for even the little while of his descent is too shameful an idea to bear. He might be followed down, in his rationalizing of the situation, by "some harmless little minx," *eine beliebige kleine Unschuld,* who might unwittingly attract a real enemy (presumably by her scent). The abstract term *Unschuld* he invests with concrete personality, in line with its grammatical gender, as a female, and its two qualifying attributes express both contempt and attraction, whereas in the phrase to follow, "some nasty little creature," *ein widerliches kleines Wesen,* only the former persists. The whole thought could stand for some trifling illicit adventure. If we remember that the heroes of Kafka's long novels yield to sexual lust under conditions to be described as unsavory by any standards, is it not surprising that the overt manifestation of the libido should have been omitted from the account of a life so filled with psychological torment as that of our hero? He refers to the distasteful female as motivated by curiosity. In its train, the fantasy of the little female leads to a second fantasy of overwhelmingly formidable proportions: supposing the very worst, there might be attracted in her wake

> someone of my own kind, some connoisseur and fancier of structures some forest vagabond, a lover of peace but a shameless bum who wants to dwell without building. If only he would come now, if only with his filthy greed he would discover the entrance, if only he would begin working to lift up the moss, if only he would succeed, if only he would wedge himself inside there for me, having got in there far enough for his hinder parts still to show for a moment, if only all this were to happen so that finally, in a mad dash after him, all inhibitions tossed aside, I could leap upon him, bite, tear, and mangle him to pieces, suck his blood to the last drop, and immediately pack his carcass with the rest of my booty, but above all—this would be the main thing—be once more in my burrow.

The terrible imagery of this wish-dream is so gripping that its motivation may dwindle into a hypnotic blank in the reader's mind. This was, indeed, my own case. Was this contingency not introduced as the most dreaded thing of all? What then transformed it in a flash into a wish-dream? It was the thought of getting home by this device, where all devices toward this end had failed, which makes him turn berserk. So all the lustful outrage is imagined as the one sure means of achieving salvation!

Of all the passages in the story, this sentence has the greatest accumulation of graphic detail. How these six steeply mounting wish-clauses reveal an escalation of passion involving voyeurism, rape, murder, and cannibalism.

After this explosion of animal passion, the speaker's tone again becomes subdued. He develops a new fixation. His favorite pastime now is to move in circles about the entrance hole, heedless of observers, playing the game of himself being the enemy that is stalking the area in order to penetrate into the inner sanctum. Now the wish to have a trusty to stand guard in his place is taken up by his imagination and developed at great length, only to be rejected because he is antisocial, and his definition of trust is a contradiction in terms. Having dismissed this line, and still finding himself prevented by a psychological block from returning home, he dreams up new ways of insuring greater safety of exit and reentry. To have two entrances instead of one, one of them very narrow, just for observation purposes, would seem a decided improvement. Its technical advantages appeal to him, but after deliberating on the pros and cons, he dismisses the whole idea in extraordinarily resolute language. The advantages are undeniable, "but only as technical achievements, not as real advantages. For, this unhindered slipping in and out, what good is it? It points to a restless disposition, to an uncertain estimation of one's own worth, to unclean appetites, bad qualities that become even worse in the face of the burrow." Every reader who is not forewarned must find it strange that this project is dismissed not on technical but on moral grounds. Five successive phrases condemn the project in the severest moral terms. The last of these phrases suggests the burrow is something hallowed and suffering desecration at the thought of such a device. After the foregoing analysis, can there be any doubt that the two entrances, very close to each other, easy to slip into and out of, suggest to the speaker specific forms of libido? Not long ago he had allowed himself to be sucked into the vortex of lustful, murderous aggression. Now that he has himself in hand again, he definitely rejects easy lubricity as a way of life.

When the tug-of-war between his yearning to return home and its compulsive interdiction is finally decided in favor of the former by a tour-de-force of autohypnosis, he does something very curious. In a trancelike daze, he detaches the cover of moss and descends. Then, remembering that he has absentmindedly forgotten to replace the cover, he reascends to the surface to correct the oversight, quite unnecessarily and quite deliberately, the word *langsam* (slowly), followed by "much too long," appearing twice in this context. This is surely a classical case of a Freudian slip (*Fehlleistung*). He blames his confusion on absentmindedness (*Zerstreutheit*)! Is he not thereby performing an exhibitionistic ritual before his final return underground?

Let us pause for a moment to summarize all the sexual anxieties we have encountered. First, in his longing to take one of the necessary excursions to the outside world, there was the inhibition against entering the maze, when he felt his pelt thinning and his fantasy pictured him as standing naked, hairless, and raw, surrounded by a mob of jeering enemies. The second, like all the following inhibitions, he faces in the world above, when the wish to reenter his burrow is blocked by the thought that his act of descending would be too conspicuous to go unnoticed. The third was a recurrence of the same fantasy expressed in poignantly emotional though veiled language, how the eyes of everyone, on the ground, in the trees, in the air, would be riveted, if only for a short moment, upon "the most precious thing I have." Number four was his fantasy of some little minx, meaning no harm, a nasty little snooper whose entering would leave her scent as a trail for the world to follow. Five: directly in the wake of this there materialized his wish-dream of one of his own kind, a male, in a posture precluding defense—the grandiosely uninhibited vision of a fellow burrower, a male marauder, whom he annihilates with berserk fury. Number six concerns his speculations about the advantages of two holes to slip in and out of at will, but these, following upon the unrestrained assertion of his overpowering libido, though technically advantageous, are rejected on moral grounds as he regains his composure. Finally, seventh, the libido, having been checked by the puritanical censor, reasserts itself in a curious Freudian slip when, in a trancelike state, having gone down into the entrance hole, he remembers that he has absentmindedly forgotten to close the trapdoor. Instead of reaching up with his paw to close it, he reemerges all the way in order to descend again, and carries out the necessary maneuver, all of this slowly and deliverately.

The return to his burrow has affected his spirits as a reviving tonic. In following his movements we are very soon struck by his use of a word that sounds odd in the mouth of a loner. The long inspection tours awaiting him are not to be rated as work, he says. Moving along those passageways is more like "a chatting with friends, the way I used to do in olden times or—I am not yet what one would really call old, but my memory has already become completely hazy as regards many things—as I used to do, or as I heard that it is usually done." As a loner he has no friends. Has he not banished from his vocabulary all memories of social intercourse? Without doubt the joy of being able to let himself go accounts for a slip of the tongue. The word "friends" (*Freunde*) having escaped his lips, he must pause with the intent of blurring it and rendering its application to his own circumstances meaningless. The syntactical twists he performs in his attempt to repudiate any admission as to erstwhile social relations of his own are a remarkable example of the inner censor at work.

The word "friends" (*Freunde*) finds us involved in the emotional climax of his homecoming. He laughs for joy and having assured himself while still outside, in sober and solemn tones, that he and his structure are one and indivisible, he now raises his voice in a paean to his tunnels and above all to his stronghold. "On your account, you tunnels and platforms, and on your account above all, my stronghold, I have come at the risk of my life, after I had long been so idiotic as to tremble on its account and delay the return to you. What do I care about the danger now that I am with you? You belong to me, I to you, we are united, what can happen to us?"

This apostrophe marks the greatest departure from the low-key approach of the story's beginning. Here for once there is a purely spontaneous flow of high-pitched joyous emotion without hedging, backtracking, or ambivalence, but this crest of the wave is of only momentary duration, for now we are on the threshold of a wholly new phase of anxiety and torment, a phase that will pursue its relentless course all the way to the point where the voice comes to a stop.

The stillness of the burrow, he has told us at the outset, was its most blissful feature, but now, after his return, something has happened to destroy this bliss. He becomes aware of a faint hissing or whistling, coming from he knows not where. Curiosity gives way to alarm. Its persistence and ubiquity are the only known elements in a multitude of unknowns which he must identify, first to account for the phenomenon and then, if possible, to remove it. We pause to note that he, the speaker, has ingeniously prepared the ground for his "psychosis," if we may use this term to denote a much more deep-seated disturbance than the anxieties that proliferated during the first half of the "story." From the start he had shown a marked anxiety regarding the continuation of the stillness. "To be sure, it is deceptive. Suddenly, at some moment, it may be broken." He also anticipated what becomes his fixation as to the cause of the noise. In commenting on the advantages deriving from the presence of the small fry in his burrow, he had checked himself to add, "Such nonchalance may perhaps not be without danger for other reasons." Is this not as if he had had an unconscious foreknowledge of both the noise and its origin? Clearly the germ of the cancer was dormant within him, biding a favorable climate to grow. When the proper moment has come to unhinge his precarious mental balance, these two built-in points are at hand for him to grasp and on which to hang, as on pegs, his psychotic hallucinations. It is as if he had, paradoxically speaking, taken out mental health insurance in reverse. As if he had known that his fundamental balance was going to be upset, he prepared in advance for local symptoms to occupy his mind and fuss over and to divert his attention from the basic issue.

Throughout the rest of the story all his ingenuity is put to work in efforts to probe into an unknown which by its nature is unknowable. His reasoning becomes overtly paranoid as one conjecture gives place to another. A remarkable illustration of this comes as he reasons, at one point, that in order to persist with the same intensity at every point of the walls and wherever he puts his ear to the ground, the sound must have two points of origin at opposite ends of his burrow. In this way, no matter how he shifts his location, the sound maintains the same degree of intensity, the diminution of one source being compensated by the augmentation of the other. Many a reader will be quick to observe that this application of the general hypothesis would hold true only if the master-builder kept moving along the straight line extending between the two poles from which the noise originates, but it is nonsensical in any case because sound does not travel at an arithmetical ratio. It is part of Kafka's peculiar humor to set such traps for the unwary reader.

The hypotheses the hero successively entertains as to the where, the how, the who, and the why of the hissing would be wearisome to recapitulate in all their turns. The extraordinarily explicit detail of their presentation serves the primary purpose of making us feel that a very long time is spent in these futile exercises of the brain. In the course of our wandering through the tortuous maze of his reasoning, we come across a couple of strikingly beautiful images regarding the stillness. Hoping to find it again he says, "It is as though the source were opening out of which the silence of the burrow flows." A little later he explores a passageway "whose stillness wakes up at my coming and envelops me from above."

The imaginative high point of emotional involvement during the process of attrition concerns "a favorite plan of my youth and maturity" (*ein Lieblingsplan meiner Jugend- und Mannes-jahre*) to hollow out a spherical area around his stronghold, leaving only a column for gravitational support to connect it with the earth. This done, he would have cavorted all over the global surface, caressing it, feeling it most intimately his own, and the delight of holding it, as it were in the hollow of his embrace, outside it, protecting it, being its guardian, would have surpassed the pleasure of being cradled inside it and enjoying its protection. Here again we happen upon that most fundamental ambivalence which provided the dominant tension during his long period of exile—the reversal of roles of protector and protégé. This is surely another manifestation of his libido, applied not to a living thing, as during his exile, but this time to his own creation. We note the ambivalence between choice of belly and womb as characteristic of his whole personality. Literally taken, this fantasy would seem to involve a total death wish, because with the ten avenues of the stronghold presumably plugged up, he would be left to perish without food and air.

It is almost embarrassing to state the obvious. During the whole declining phase of his life, that is, after his return to the burrow, the hero is the victim of a haunting hallucination. We note that the paranoid, ever-present preoccupation with the sound, while taking the predominant form of theoretical explanation, also expresses itself in senseless and self-destructive activity. Exasperated by the elusiveness of the noise, he claws at the walls of his tunnels, digging holes at random and reducing the beautifully smooth design of his passageways to a shambles. Realizing the self-destructive futility of these acts at last, he resolves, as the preliminary to another grandiose and harebrained thrust into the unknown, to repair the damage; but to the extent that he sets about doing so, instead of merely thinking about the project, his heart is not in the work. He performs it listlessly as though under the eyes of a foreman (*Aufseher*). How things have changed again! For all its drudgery, the work of executing his blueprint was the self-imposed goal of self-glorification; now he feels reduced to the status of an employee, laboring reluctantly under another's direction.

The long phase of paranoid hallucination takes a new turn when, not far from the end of the story, he seeks to escape from the haunting sound by approaching the maze, threading his way through its labyrinthine walls, and settling down inside the exit hole. By another ambivalent turn, the din of the world's traffic outside affords relief to his harassed mind from the obsession of the hissing sound. Here he can concentrate afresh on theorizing as to the trouble within. By all odds, the most remarkable theory to which he now attaches himself is that of a monstrously large and powerful animal, ploughing its way through the earth at a swinging stride, spirally encircling the burrow to which it has already drawn nearer by several loops. The hissing he interprets as nothing but the echoing tremor of his relentless approach. "Someone is coming." (*Es kommt jemand heran.*) The symbolism of this projection as the inescapable doom of death is too obvious for us to miss. But instead of his facing it for what it is, it awakens in him a memory of his adolescent days when his work on the burrow was still tentative and subject to change. He remembers having heard the sound of a fellow burrower. At that time he responded to it with curiosity mixed with indifference, but without fear. The noise would alternately be felt as nearer or more distant, and there came a time when he no longer heard it. During all of that time he was equally prepared to face an intruder in a clean-cut fight, or to move his own operations to an area where he would not be disturbed by neighbors.

To us, this reminiscence shows the difference between the sound mind of the vigorous adolescent and the diseased mind of the creature grown old. Ironically, he puts a different interpretation upon it. "Admonitions were not wanting." (*An Mahnungen hat es nicht gefehlt.*) He sees this incident of his youth as a warning, an admonition which he should have heeded in order to avoid the inexorable burrower who will be getting him at last. The term "admonitions" (*Mahnungen*) is one of those peculiar words that induces us to gather up the threads of what we sense as a religious element of his experiences. We remember that casual but altogether enigmatic remark about his protective devices having worked "by way of exception, by way of grace, because Providence has a special stake in the preservation of my forehead, the stamping-hammer," where he voiced his conviction that he enjoyed the special protection of Providence, and claimed a relationship of interdependence with it. The level of this wording left it an open question whether this expressed the buoyancy of youthful genius, a whimsical bit of pragmatic philosophy, a cynical witticism, or the deep conviction of a mystical bond obtaining between him and higher powers. During his prolonged exile there emerged a feeling regarding his structure as radiating a mystical power to keep him from harm, exempting him, as he then put it, from the universal struggle for survival.

Now, with the word "admonitions" still sounding in our ears, we listen to a series of rhetorical questions, couched in the language of genuine religious emotion: "How did it happen that for so long a time tranquillity and happiness pervaded my burrow? Who was it that guided the paths of my enemies that they skirted my domain by a great curve? Why was I protected so long only to be so terrorized now?" This is the conversion (*das Insichgehen*) of the repentant sinner, humbly acknowledging the error of his ways in having turned a deaf ear to divine guidance. We ask the question: are all these successive stages of a religious turn of mind to be interpreted as progressive phases of a mind coming apart? Whatever one may think of Kafka's own religious development, the religious factor in the context of this story must be taken as a symptom of a progressive mental deterioration. This humility is not old age mellowing to wisdom; it is the pragmatism of a creature grown bewildered and feeble. To put it another way: the pragmatism of self-conscious youth has yielded to a senile will-to-believe.

Only one short phase remains to be reviewed. Lying just below the moss cover of the exit vent, separated from his tunnels and the central stronghold by the maze, he again feels the urge to betake himself off. Subject as always to the tension of ambivalent desires, he wishes he were too feeble to respond to the homing urge. He does get back to the stronghold. Now he speculates on the guidelines that should have dictated its construction. From the outset he has referred to it in terms of defense; the word *Verteidigung* has frequently occurred in this context. However, we must have felt all along, supposing that we gave any thought to the matter, that what he calls his *Burgplatz*—rendered by us as stronghold—is a grandiose misnomer. It is a place of shelter and protection and its spaciousness would make it a fine status symbol if its possessor were part of any social order, in the absence of which it is an expression of self-aggrandizement. But of defensive devices in the proper sense of the word there is not a trace. This insight has come to him very late and he now thinks of guidelines to be translated into engineering know-how for the purpose of confusing and annihilating a potential foe. But self-criticism has long ceased to have any relation to practical initiative. The dissociation of theoretical reason from practical living, of the brain from the body, is complete. Barren introspection has totally replaced reason in the service of life. From the vantage point of a higher perspective, as he now realizes, all his life has been play. Fear being everpresent, he deliberates on the chances of negotiating with an intruder, but he still has sense enough to realize that his proposals are silly. Things finally boil down to a single item of animal instinct: let him reduce the store of his supplies by consuming as much as possible while there is time. We see him last, in his mutilated stronghold, under a pile of rubble with a piece of flesh between his teeth. He has stopped talking. His last sentence, though complete enough, could have involved an about-face. But for all practical purposes he is finished, his life and strength are played out. We may think of him as having died in his sleep, without any conscious struggle. Confrontation, torture, and pain are related to strength. This speaker's strength is gone.

There is a final question to be answered: is "The Burrow" complete or is it a fragment? Many critics, Emrich among them, hedge their answer by referring to the assertion of Kafka's friends, Max Brod and Dora Dymant, that there was to be an encounter which would have ended with the hero's death. Pasley, who had the benefit of Kafka's manuscript in preparing his college edition, asserts that the final page is completely filled without any terminating punctuation mark. This he takes as proof that there was more to follow. There is the fact, moreover, pointed out to me by Professor Steven Scher, that in Pasley's version, the last four words are separated from what precedes by a mere semicolon, whereas Max Brod's heavy-handed editing saw fit to set them off by a period and a dash. Now it is perfectly conceivable that the hero might have gone on verbalizing for a number of paragraphs, but it is difficult to imagine what more he could have had to say. If, as I believe, Kafka thought of his hero as destined to die of a heart attack or other natural causes, he could have snapped his life cord right then and there by stopping his pen in the middle of the last word of the final phrase, but he did not choose to do so.

But what of the alleged violent confrontation that was to end the hero's life? This is improbable, even impossible, on a variety of grounds. To begin with, the ruminations of our hero regarding the relentless approach of a silent predator can be dismissed as the figments of a feverishly hallucinating brain. Beyond this, surveying our hero's whole life span, we find not a single instance of any overt attempt on the part of any living creature to invade his stronghold. To introduce such an event now, when the burrower's life has entered its twilight zone, would be tantamount to using the device of a freak chance to end matters—a device contrary to all esthetic logic and unworthy of Kafka.

But the idea of a terminal fight is untenable on other grounds. Have we forgotten that this "story" unfolds as the synchronous reeling off of the hero's life and his voice? He has talked his life away without any break in the flow: But how could he continue to speak with his teeth engaged in snapping at his opponent's throat? In other words, the author would have been compelled at a certain point to introduce the voice of a second speaker, the voice of the "omniscient author." Such an abrupt change of focus is unthinkable in the sophisticated atmosphere of Kafka's art.

Is there, then, no possibility of any definitive ending to a story built on such premises? No creature, however miraculously endowed or engineered, can report on its own death. Very well; but I think there is a way of contriving to have the hero speak to his very last heartbeat and for us to know that it is his last. Suppose we let him experience his death by heart failure to an accompanying nightmare. This could have been put into words that finally echo from the land of no return. Seizing Kafka's pen, we have the temerity to write:

> Da, was ist das? Geräusch das mich aufschreckt und mich zwingt die Augen aufzuschlagen. Aus der zerschlissenen Wand hervor, mir entgegen, schiebt sich ein riesiges Gebiß, und in dem ich den Abgrund seines dunklen Schlundes hinuntergleite, höre ich noch das Knacken meiner Kniescheiben und Knöchel zwischen seinen Kiefern.

> There, what's that? A noise that startles and forces me to open my eyes. Out of the crumbling wall there reaches toward me an enormous set of jaws, and as I feel myself slide down the dark abyss of his gullet, I can hear the crackling of my kneecaps and ankles between his grinders.

Since Kafka did not give this version the sanction of his Imprimatur, choosing rather the ambiguity of open-endedness, "the rest is silence."

Rebecca West

Kafka and the Mystery of Bureaucracy

It is almost impossible to study Kafka as a great writer should be studied. His production is too incoherent. He was for most of his life ill and often in pain; he died at the age of forty-one in 1924, which meant that he had lived through a hideous historical crisis; he was terrified by intimation that another and more hideous crisis was to come; he was exposed to a disintegrating-intellectual climate. Hence his writings are in themselves disorderly, most of them mere sketches and beginnings, and he handled them with the carelessness of a sick man; and even the major works are so feverishly taken up and set aside that the sequence of chapters in one of his two masterpieces, *The Trial,* is uncertain. When he died he took no measures for the preservation of his writings, but on the contrary ordered their destruction, and it is only to the disobedience of his friend Max Brod that we owe our knowledge of them. Of the papers he left, many were seized by the Nazis, long after his death, and are lost. It is therefore necessary, in considering his work, to abandon sometimes the simple duty of the reader to attend to what he wrote, and take it that that must be what he meant, and instead to guess at his meaning, often by reference to his personal life.

. . . Kafka's title to immortality lies in his two long works *The Trial* and *The Castle,* his short story "In the Penal Colony," many short passages which (though they are sometimes embedded in short stories) present a thought or impression complete in itself, and a number of aphorisms. His novel *Amerika* and some other short stories are entertaining, but they are not of great moment.

Both *The Trial* and *The Castle* present us with a chain of mysterious

Reprinted from The Yale Review. *Copyright © Yale University Press. By permission of Yale University Press. This essay appears in Rebecca West's* The Court *and* The Castle *(New Haven, Conn.: Yale University Press, 1957).*

events which are never explained in rational terms. *The Trial* describes the last days of a bank clerk who was suddenly visited by some warders and told that he was charged with a crime, never defined, by a court of which he has never heard, which has no recognized courtroom, and of which people seem to have only a sort of folkloric knowledge. "K." more and more realizes that by all standards of human justice, he is the victim of injustice, and that the court's dealings with him are clumsy, inefficient, and cruel, above all in its refusal to give him the least hint of the charge that is being made against him. Yet the whole pattern of events makes him feel more and more that he is indeed guilty, and that there is a way of looking at this injustice which would reveal it as absolute justice. In the end he is executed for his crime, without the pretense of a fair trial. *The Castle* is the story of a land surveyor, who is also called by the initial of Kafka's own surname, who arrives in a village to take up a position to which he believes he has been appointed by an authority housed in a great castle which overlooks the village. But he cannot himself get in touch with the castle, for any attempts he makes to communicate with it are rebuffed; and all that happens is that various officials send down messages suggesting that the appointment has not really been made, and that anyway there is no need for the services of any land surveyor in the neighborhood. The wretched man drags on his days, surrounded by hostile or at least derisive villagers, his hopes occasionally stimulated by messages from the castle which suggest that perhaps he was appointed after all, perhaps his services would be valuable, and had the book ever been finished we were to see him die in this state of uncertainty, which is the more bewildering because he comes toward the end to feel that perhaps the castle has reason for its attitude.

It is important to understand that these fantastic stories are not fantasies. They have a realistic basis, and they strain belief only because Kafka was looking at an institution about which he knew more than most people and about which he had a completely objective but ardent feeling, so that he set down the best and the worst about it with an intensity usually associated with prejudice. For these books are on one level about bureaucracy, as *Hamlet* is on one level about the affairs of the royal family of Elsinore, though on a deeper level they are, like *Hamlet,* about the soul of man and his prospects of salvation and damnation. Kafka knew a very great deal about bureaucracy. He was brought up under the highly bureaucratic political system of the Habsburg Empire, and he lived his mature life under the democratized bureaucracy of Czechoslovakia. It is to be noted that the bureaucracy of Europe is an impressive institution, particularly in Eastern Europe. It is said that the civil service in that area enjoys a special prestige because the fathers of that service were the scribes who acted as intermediaries between the kings and princes of the aboriginal peoples in their dealings with the barbarian invaders. The civil service had also, in more recent ages, a special value to the population, for when a peasant or artisan family produced an intellectual, he could go into the priesthood, or take up a profession, or, if he wanted to avoid the limitations of the ecclesiastical life and the insecurity of professional life, become a civil servant. This became an even more useful social resource when Maria Theresa opened the civil service to her Jewish subjects. The consumer also was in favor of the institution, for it operated efficiently enough in spite of the many jests at its *Schlamperei,* and it covered a large territory with a network of social services which did in fact protect the interests of most of the population, and met nearly all eventualities. The inhabitant of the Habsburg Empire had great reason to feel gratitude to its bureaucracy. But that it was reasonable to feel such gratitude provoked a conflict of a complicated nature in any man placed as Kafka was.

He was a Jew living in the Czech division of the Empire, then called Bohemia. The Czechs did not wish to be part of the Empire, which was dominated by Austrian Germans and Magyars, whereas they were Slavs, with all the Slav passion for independence. Therefore they resented the Habsburg law and bureaucracy, even when these worked well; but the German inhabitants rejoiced in them. The Jews ranged themselves with the Germans, because the Habsburgs had treated the Jews well on the whole, and also because they were suspicious of the Czechs, precisely because they were anti-German, and because they were Slavs and kin to the great Slav power Russia, which was then the most anti-Semitic power in existence. The Jews' relation to Russia was not only hostile but shamefaced. Russia was the promoter of pogroms and the maintainer of ghettos, and it had succeeded in oppressing its Jews till they had become nightmare figures which the Western Jews did not like to recognize as brethren, since, isolated and terrorized, shut up with their religion in a state of tension which revived all their primitive fantasies, they had become at once barbaric and pedantic. Inevitably the Jews of Prague were driven back to the Germans; but the Germans were often anti-Semitic.

Kafka was acutely conscious of this dilemma. He related to Gustav Janouch, a Gentile who was for a brief period his Eckerman, how the Prague Jewish poet Oskar Baum had as a little boy attended the German primary school where there were frequent fights between the German and Czech pupils. During one of these, little Baum was hit over the head by a Czech child with a pencil-box so hard that he sustained a detached retina and lost his sight. Kafka said: "The Jew Oskar Baum lost his sight as a German, although in fact he never was one, and no Germans would have accepted him as one. Perhaps Oskar is merely a melancholy symbol of the so-called German Jews of Prague."[1] There was therefore the paradox that Jews, by the mere fact of acting as loyal Austrian citizens and upholding the Habsburg law, might cause outbreaks of lawlessness; and it must be remembered that this was not a merely local predicament, for the heart of the Empire had been profoundly influenced at that time by the demagogics of its famous burgomaster Karl Lueger, who was an apostle of anti-Semitism. The Habsburg law that the Jews respected was therefore hostile to the Jewish law, to which they paid more than respect. To many people this would have meant that they had to choose which of the two laws they would uphold and which they would repudiate or consider of secondary importance. But Kafka was not a rebel. It was part of his doctrine that the time had come to conform. However much the Habsburg law and the Jewish law might conflict, he meant to uphold them both. The reconciliation of opposites, of making consistencies out of inconsistencies, was, therefore, a familiar idea to him.

When he grew up he became a member of the staff of the Workmen's Accident Assurance Association, and, irritable though he was, and artist though he was, he did not rebel even at the actual routine of bureaucracy. He lamented that it left him so little time for his own writing, but he bowed to the social importance of his work; and in time he came to write the following letter to a woman he loved, who had begged him to tell a lie and get leave of absence to spend some time with her:

> I can't come because I can't tell a lie to the office. I can lie to the office, but only for two reasons, out of fear (it's actually an office privilege, it belongs to it, there I tell lies unprepared, by heart, inspired) or out of dire necessity (for instance, supposing it were "Elsa ill," Elsa, Elsa—not you, Milena, you don't fall ill, that would be direct necessity, of this I won't even talk) thus out of necessity I could lie at once, then no telegram would be needed. Necessity can get by in the office. In this case I leave either with or without permission. But in all cases where, among the reasons that I would have for lying, happiness, the necessity for happiness, is the main reason, there I cannot lie, can do it as little as I can lift two Kg. dumb-bells. If I came to the Director with the Elsa-telegram, it would certainly drop out of my hand, and if it fell I would certainly step on it, on the lie, and having done that, I would certainly run away from the Director without having asked for anything. You must realize, Milena, that the office is not just any old stupid institution (though it is this too, and superabundantly, but that is not the point, as a matter of fact, it is more fantastic than stupid) but it has been my life up to

[1] Gustav Janouch, *Conversations with Kafka* (New York: Praeger, 1953), p.67.

now, I cannot tear myself away from it, though perhaps this wouldn't be so bad, but up to now it has been my life, I can treat it shabbily, work less than anyone else (which I do), botch the work (which I do), can in spite of it make myself important (which I do), can calmly accept as due to me the most considerate treatment imaginable in an office—but lie, in order to travel suddenly as a free man, being after all only an employed official, to a place where "nothing else" but my natural heartbeat drives me—well, in this way I cannot lie. But one thing I wanted to tell you even before I received your letter—that right away this week I'll try to get my passport renewed or otherwise made valid so that I can come at once if it has to be.

. . . Perhaps it's more difficult for me to tell lies in the office than for someone (and most officials are like this) who is convinced he is unfairly treated, that he works beyond his capacity—if only I had this conviction it would almost mean an express train to Vienna—someone who considers the office to be a stupidly run machine—which he would run much better—a machine in which, owing to the management's stupidity, he is employed in the wrong place—according to his abilities he should be an upper-upper-wheel and here he has to work as an upper-under-wheel and so on, but to me the office—and so was elementary school, grammar school, university, family, everything—to me the office is a living person who looks at me wherever I am with his innocent eyes, a person with whom I'm connected in some way unknown to myself, although he's stranger to me than the people whom at this moment I hear crossing the Ring in their automobiles. He is strange to the point of absurdity, but just this requires consideration, I make hardly any effort to conceal my being a stranger, but when does such innocence recognize this—in a word: I cannot lie.[2]

This is, of course, a modern version of "I could not love thee, Dear, so much Loved I not honor more." But it is more than that. Here was a man who was feeling for the bureaucratic system in which he lived something like the emotion which Shakespeare felt for the monarchy. But like Shakespeare he was clear-eyed for all his loyalty, and he knew the worst about the object of his loyalty. A storm of blood and misery has raged over Eastern Europe since his time; but these two letters have survived.

To Herr Dr. Franz Kafka, clerk in Prague V, Mikulasska tr 36. You are required to answer the communication from this office, dated 25th September 1922, Rp 38/21, within eight days. In the event of

---

[2] Franz Kafka, *Letters to Milena*, pp. 127-128.

your failure to do so the matter will be referred to District Finance Headquarters, Prague, and you will become liable to payment of a fine.[3]

To the Revenue Department, Zizhov, Prague. Your enquiry of the— has already been answered by me, not verbally, because I am seriously ill, but on a postcard and immediately. The card was certainly delivered, for some time later I received from your Department an enquiry as to what I was referring to on that card, there being no record at your office of any summons dated 25th September 1922 Rp 38/21. In order to avoid complicating this matter, as completely unimportant to the Revenue Department as to myself, I did not answer this second enquiry, incidentally wishing to save postage; if the original letter of the—, was no longer on your files, I was quite justified in letting it go at that. But since the matter has now been revived by your communication of the 3rd November and I am now, in spite of having long ago answered in a correct manner, even being threatened with a fine, I should like to inform you again that since Paul Hermann's entry into the firm of First Prague Asbestos Works no further investments have been made by the partners and that the firm ceased to exist in March 1917. I hope that this time my answer will reach the department concerned.[4]

The confusion of which this is an example is often uproariously funny, and is obviously not so catastrophic as the beheadings and tortures and imprisonments that are the byproducts of more primitive systems of government. But it may result in suffering dire enough. A clerk may be unjustly accused of inefficiency and lose promotion, a sick man may be called from his bed to serve in the army, an old man may suddenly have his pension cut off and starve. It is therefore possible for Kafka to see the bureaucracy of which he was a part as beneficent, comic, murderously cruel, and absolutely necessary. (This is, of course, what Shakespeare thought about the monarchy.) That vision of the bureaucracy undoubtedly inspires both *The Trial* and *The Castle,* which must be read as satires on the subject. But there are three reasons for considering them as having another and more important significance.

The first reason is objective: both books contain material impossible to relate to bureaucratic affairs. The most devoted civil servant would admit that the atmosphere of Whitehall or the Pentagon does not accord with the solemnity of the cathedral chapter in *The Trial,* and that the execution scene at the end of the book does not correspond with any part of normal office routine; and there is nothing in any known bureau-

[3] Franz Kafka, *Wedding Preparations* (Ernest Kaiser and Edith Wilkins, trans.) (London: Secker and Warburg Ltd., 1954), p. 445.
    [4] *Ibid.,* pp. 428-429.

cratic system which exactly corresponds with the strange collection of women found in the village in *The Castle*. Frieda and Olga and Amalia and Pepi might conceivably be members of a typists' pool, but the two landladies of the inns resist classification. The second reason is also objective: Kafka was deeply concerned with religion, and it would be odd if he wrote two books in which he dealt with ideas so closely associated with religious thought as guilt and punishment and redemption, and kept his mind exclusively on bureaucracy. The third reason is subjective and to be breathed with caution: many persons who read these books experience strong emotions of a kind unlikely to be aroused by the satirical treatment of bureaucracy, and find that they awaken associations of a philosophical and religious nature.

Both books can be interpreted as religious allegories. It is possible to regard K. in *The Trial* as not only a bank clerk who gets involved with a piece of state machinery which he does not understand, but a soul laboring under the conviction of having sinned against God. His rational self asks what sin it is that he has committed, because he has kept the laws of man faithfully, and longs to seek God and ask Him how He dares find him, or any other man, guilty of sin when He created the sinner and gave him the opportunity to sin. It is also possible to regard K. in *The Castle* not simply as a land surveyor who cannot do his work because the authority which employs him has got into a muddle, but as a soul who is anxious to serve God but who cannot find out what it is that God wills him to do, nor even how to conceive God. In both books K. wants to look upon the face of God and fails; and there is here a correspondence with the lot of modern man, who when he looks at the social power which shapes his material destiny, looks not at a king but at a faceless democracy. But it is not to be taken for granted that Kafka justifies the ways of God to man, that he accepts either the spiritual or social world. The end of *The Trial* describes how K. is taken from his home by his two executioners, in a state of consent to his own death. He knows that in some sense he is not innocent. The executioners take him to a place outside the town where there is an abandoned quarry with a house standing beside it, they lay him down on the ground, they take out a long butcher's knife. As he is stabbed the casements of a window in the top story of the house fly open, someone leans over the sill and stretches out his arms. There is a sense of someone watching who is on his side; and the executioners have folded up K.'s clothes "as if they were likely to be used again at some time, though perhaps not immediately." There is thus a promise of resurrection, but the last words of the book are bitter beyond any sweetening. " 'Like a dog!' he said; it was as if the shame of it must outlive him." Could eternity ever wipe out the humiliation of time? Could man ever be at peace with a God who had forced him to endure life?

The Castle contains a like admission of man's guilt followed by a counterattack on God. When the land surveyor arrives in the village to take up the post to which the Castle has appointed him, the Castle takes up an equivocal position, sometimes denying this and sometimes admitting it, and doing nothing whatsoever to protect him from the villagers' hostility. It is to be noted that Kafka suggests sometimes that K. has in fact been appointed and sometimes that he is an able but unscrupulous man who wants this appointment and hopes he may get it by pretending he has got it. Thus he is shown as both the king and the usurper; and as the spiritual parallels of the king and the usurper are different phases of the same man, this is apparent nonsense and real sense. The king is man at any given moment; the usurper is that same man who, discontented with his state, performs an act of will, and changes himself. But in the end K. admits that the castle was in any case right. He says to Pepi the chambermaid (p. 378):

> It is as if we had both striven too intensively, too noisily, too child-ishly, with too little experience, to get something that for instance with Frieda's calm and Frieda's matter-of-factness can be got easily and without much ado. We have tried to get it by crying, by scratch-ing, by tugging—just as a child tugs at the tablecloth, gaining nothing, but only bringing all the splendid things down on the floor and putting them out of its reach for ever.

He means, surely, that they had lacked what Keats called "Negative cap-ability, that is, when a man is capable of being in uncertainties, mys-teries, doubts, without any irritable reaching after fact and reason." To that degree K. is shown to be at fault. Yet the village women in *The Castle* make an accusation against God. All of them are involved in love affairs with the officials in the castle, principally with the very important Herr Klamm, who seems to be the permanent under-secretary; and so much is this approved that one woman, Amalia, is universally scorned because, on receiving a brutally indecent summons from an official who had seen her at a festival, she tore it up and closed her window on the messenger. To understand this curious situation, it must be realized that Kafka had a great distaste for sex, even greater than Shakespeare's. "Love," he once remarked, "always appears hand in hand with filth," and he was therefore forced to regard women as involved in evil, although he rec-ognized that the material world could not survive without sex and women. He had to face the fact that God had committed Himself to a scheme for the human race which involved imperfection, and of a peculiarly gross kind. Kafka was willing to admit that God must be right, and that explains the episode of Amalia. She is considered a sinner for refusing the indecent summons of the official because she was thereby refusing to coöperate with the Divine Will on the ground that it did not conform with human standards of decorum. Frieda, on the other hand, who has been Klamm's mistress, enjoys the peace of acceptance, which for Kafka was a paradox. But it is not certain that Kafka ever found a way of reconciling himself to the strange decree of God that such impurity should be necessary. This may be why he left the book unfinished.

Kafka thought of the will of man as corrupt with a corruption even fouler than Shakespeare ever ascribed to it; and he thought a little better of the court than Shakespeare did, for if it reeked of corrupting humanity it was also part of a divine plan which occasionally oriented it toward salvation. But all this was not of final consequence, for God would redeem the soul of man and gather it to Him in eternity, and the court would pass away, as all things which belong to time. This is a not unusual religious opinion, and it illustrates the curious dislocation of modern thought that many people find it astonishing that a major imaginative writer should have been inspired by it, and can hardly believe that that is what Kafka meant. It is also true that Kafka makes his point obscurely, because of a conscious decision he made regarding method. He rebelled against the spawning of characters which was choking the brooks of fiction with fish not worth the taking; and he would have liked to write a novel so far as possible without the use of character, concentrating on the development of a theme. Janouch says that he asked Kafka if the characters of Rossman and the Stoker, in the story named "The Stoker," which was afterward incorporated in *Amerika,* were drawn from life, and Kafka answered impatiently, "I was not describing people, I was telling a story, these characters are only images, symbols."

Peter Dow Webster

"Dies Irae" in the Unconscious, or the Significance of Franz Kafka

The Kafka problem has become the Kafka quarrel. Critics and readers alike, moved within by forces they deny or reluctantly admit, offer the most diverse responses to the writings and life of one who specialized in his own neurosis and its bewildering consequences. Since he speaks with great penetration of his own problem as a psycho-neurotic, and since there is so much of Kafka's vestigial infantilism in all of us, since as men we are all guilty, the critics have explored his symbolism to reconstruct the inner man from his works. An expert in the artistic creation of fantasy, Kafka suggests the psychoanalyst turned artist. If Edmund Spenser is the poet's poet, then Franz Kafka is the psychologist's perfect dreamer. The *Dies Irae* he reveals in the unconscious as it accuses, tries, and condemns the conscious is an ironical reversal of civilized man's complacent assumption that his ego is a free or significant agent in contacting reality. It is almost mirthful to read Sigmund Freud's dream that where id is, there shall ego be. The problems are many; the critics generally separated into the naturalistic and religious groups. The central issue, as you become one of the jury, is: "Who committed this ancient wrong?"

So perfect is Kafka the artist in projecting this neurosis in the Freudian symbolism and dream-distortion technique that we ourselves are stirred to participate in the dream. We become alert for every sign of the original wound, for the anger of the rejected, insecure, infantile ego, for the displacement of this hate upon itself, for its sense of guilt and unworthiness, its shame, its magnification of the aggressor in fantasy, its helpless terror.

From College English *(October 1950), Vol. 12, No. 1, pp. 9-15. Copyright 1950 by the National Council of Teachers of English. Reprinted by permission of the publisher.*

In all of this there is a curiously disturbing detachment. It is as though Kafka were both the dreamer and the spectator of his dreams. No morality such as we know in real life intervenes between the dreamer and his dream. It is a world without actual persons, events, or obstacles. Only the past of the dreamer is strangely active, and the childish fantasy forever dominates the adolescent or mature perspective of things-as-they-should-be. *Alice in Wonderland* is a great fantasy; *Pilgrim's Progress* is a very great allegory; *The Trial* is the projection into the form of fantasy of the reality within an obstructed psyche, a mind divided against itself. The humor of the dream is here; you can sense the displacement, the isolation, the absurd quality of the whole business. The trouble is, you can't dismiss it from your mind. It is a dream that haunts and in a shadowy way reflects the shadows within.

Was Franz Kafka really seeking his indestructible Self? Or did he only think he was? Was his aggressive defiance of the "infant father" the center, the core of his being? Is his real sin the unwillingness to grow up or the inability of an already atrophied personality to face the reality within and without simultaneously? Was his mature shame—his feeling that he had only fooled himself, his sense of having wasted his life in a struggle to preserve the ignoble part of his being—a really calm and wise judgment of the issues in the battle he lost or was it but a reflection within the ego of the humiliation, the masochism, he inflicted in self-punishment upon himself for having willed the death of his father? Was he psychologically predetermined to the conflict by his nervous system, his very weakness of organization necessitating an unusual degree of security with the mother and fear of the father, or did the self within become polluted through a jealousy and rage for which the mature personality must assume responsibility and which it can negate by conscious redirection? How much can psychoanalysis really activate in the counseling of Dr. Huld, the advocate of the court and pleader for the self-doomed Joseph K.? When you answer these questions, there are countless others.

When we say that his psyche is divided, we are using the same figure of speech Christ used in the "house divided against itself." It is not a fixed status but a dynamic relation characterized by changing degrees of tension, distress, suspicion, fear, and aggression of separately motivated centers within the total self. The three circles are not in consonant flow but get in the way of each other. Instead of being in harmony with his past and his present, Kafka is snagged by his infantile fantasies, which remain dominant because they have never been adequately discharged of their cathexis. Not that anyone is ever completely free. As the court painter, Titorelli, points out, there are only legendary stories of definitive acquittal. The best one can hope for, if he faces the issue squarely, adjusts himself to the present state of affairs, is either ostensible acquittal or indefinite postponement. Once you are on trial, as Leni tells our hero, Joseph K., the best thing to do is to admit guilt and throw yourself on the mercy of the court. For the unconscious is always right. There are no errors (except Freudian slips) in the court of the unconscious. So here is Joseph K., bank assessor, aged thirty, suddenly arrested and seeking for justice as an innocent man; all he wants is his rights, and he can't even see the judge or know what the specifications of his crime are. It is all absurd because the worlds of ego-value and of unconscious truth are not brought into line. Reason must accept unreason; the world within is a world of incommensurables.

For Titorelli in *The Trial* is the painter of the court; he is the maker of unconscious fantasies. He is in a way the private painter of Joseph K.'s succession of emotional experiences; and yet his technique is inherited, and he might as well have been painting a thousand years ago. He learned his trade from his father, and everything he paints must be painted just so. It makes no difference how the judge actually looked; he is going to look a certain way when Titorelli has finished the job by order. It is all in classic style, and the unconscious, which is all that really matters anyhow, knows what these symbols mean. The judges, who decide your case without reference to your plea (for how can the conscious make any impression on the unconscious?), must be interviewed by advocates (psychoanalysts), who understand the symbols of the unconscious. The uninstructed ego is like a child in the presence of inscrutable wisdom and power. But the really important thing is that everyone gets justice. There are no errors. The court is absolutely right. This is the apparently arbitrary power that interferes with a man just when he is going places in the world of business. How stupid to feel this fatigue, anxiety, and shame. If it were a problem that really mattered—at the bank, Joseph K. would show who he was and what he could do. This is like the sense of futility and terror, of absurdity and infinite sorrow, that Poe felt when his unconscious, in the form of a "grim, ungainly, ghastly, gaunt, and ominous bird of yore," stepped across the threshold and remained perched above the bust of Pallas just above his chamber door. It has been the experience of millions and will be of millions more as the childish fantasy retained in the unconscious conflicts with the adjustment of the ego to reality.

What Kafka does in *The Trial* is to narrate with perfect detachment the symbolic sequence of past libido-fantasies in conflict with everything the persona wants to be and think and do. Now Joseph K., our hero, enters the realm of unconscious memories in the studio of a painter who is both a father-surrogate and a dynamic image-maker fixated on the anal level. He enters the studio, of course, from his present point in time. Here is adolescent or mature sex drive, already crippled by the past it is seeking and by which it is also bound. At this stage, Joseph K. knows sex only as furtive prostitution, and the feeling-tone is projected onto the leader of the group of girls who accompany him up the stairs to the studio of unconscious memories. Titorelli is in his nightshirt, as we would expect him to be. Infantile fantasies have already assaulted Joseph K. in an almost revolting scene at the entrance to the studio, and the past and present are interwoven in the action which follows. Adolescent libido is locked out, though the girls are greatly amused and want to enter the studio. The action is reversed as in a dream, and the girls function in answer to the effort that Joseph K. is making toward complete heterosexuality, completely genitalized. Of all the surprising things in this nonsensical world, the girls also belong to the court. Can you imagine that! Well, it is the secret for which Joseph K. had been looking, with the forward thrust of the libido, while he was fixated on the lower, anal level. Does he recognize its significance? No. Why? Because the really significant thing in a dream is always suggested as an incidental, a thing of no account at all. Titorelli's pointed statement is followed up as information by a remark that strips it of all disturbing significance. Read the rest of the scene and see how perfect its symbolism is.

But at the end, the dream having revealed its all, the old child in the mature Joseph takes over. Given his choice of going out of the studio of unconscious memory by the door behind the bed or the door behind which the girls (hilariously stupid and meaningful) were waiting, Joseph goes out through childhood fantasy, where again the imagery is that of the child wondering about the source, not the fulfillment, of his being. And all he takes away is his own fixation. He buys ever so many pictures of "Wild Nature, a Heathscape," all with the same two stunted trees, some darkish grass, and a sunset. Even Titorelli points out that Joseph K. just loves depressing pictures. He takes them back to his office in the bank and locks them up in a bottom drawer of his desk. He is now going to pay attention to things that really matter. This is the humor, the satire, the direction, the wisdom of the dream trying to make the dreamer's condition known to him. For the dream itself is but a shadow in which the past and the present are perfectly interwoven. To understand the significance of this chapter is to be prepared for the complete stupidity of Joseph K. in his next and final session with the advocate, whom he dismisses with tragic nonchalance. Joseph K. is one of the men who must die because they cannot or will not wait until favorable contact is made with their unconscious. I need not recall for those who have read Brod that throughout this period Kafka was making and breaking a formal engagement with F. B., and that the Fräulein Bürstner of *The Trial* is the artistic appropriation of the girl in the flesh.

Chapter nine of *The Trial* has been the happy hunting ground of all the cabals. Critics read it and talk about it as though it were not an integral part of the story of Joseph K.'s arrest, trial, search, and death. Critics find in it a satire on the ecclesiastical cabala, an exposé of its mumbo-jumbo, and even an allegory of some kind of undefined but tremendously transcendental truth. As in the scene with the painter, we are again in the realm of Joseph K.'s inner world. And the only incommensurable elements are the fantasies of the unconscious in the presence of the ego and its canons of logic. It is of the same texture as the rest of *The Trial* and completes the story of Joseph K.'s inquiry before the court's verdict is executed upon him.

Though a Czech Jew by birth, Kafka had only the cursory form of the Judaic faith, picked up incidentally in the formal celebration of the principal holidays. He was irked by his father's hypocrisy and lack of faith. Even though he had been taught its glorious faith, he could not have found its peace and beauty until he had forgiven his own father, been reconciled to his father, and been born again, heir to the promises and the covenant made with Abraham. Whatever the explanation may be, probably a further attempt to escape his father as fantasy created in infancy, Kafka, like Freud, wanted to belong to the majority group, sought faith through the medium of Kierkegaard's work, but, doomed by his own unconscious, repudiated the general neurosis as cure for the private neurosis. The symbolism of the cathedral scene is outwardly Christian, but the parable of the man from the country and the doorkeeper of the law has an unmistakably Judaic tone.

Just before he leaves the conscious for the unconscious, Leni, that lovely little maid who waited on the advocate, Dr. Huld, calls by phone, learns where he is going, and with pity in her voice says: "They're driving you hard." As symbolic of the Eve that Joseph K. carried in his heart, he found her unexpected sympathy almost more than he could bear. For the cathedral is again the unconscious, but the most dreaded of all aspects of the unconscious—the religious. Here is the last chance to prevent the unknown from remaining forever unknowable. Here is the chance to save one's life by losing it, to achieve the indestructible in one's self by entering through that one door prepared for Joseph K. alone. For Kafka knew that, although there were a thousand places of refuge, there was only one place of salvation. But it is Joseph K.'s conscious that is flowing down into the universal womb of the unconscious, whence he might have been born again but was not.

It is always a particular man or ego that comes into the Presence. It is always the personal self that one has protected from invasion, from the *tremendum*. The selected details and attitudes are perfect. Joseph sees the old woman kneeling before the Madonna. He sees the verger lighting the candles on the altar. It grows dark. One tall, thick candle on the pillar makes the darkness more visible. He moves as in a dream to a small adjacent chapel, where he is metamorphosed in dream magic into an errant knight, leaning on his sword, which is stuck into the bare ground; and he stands there as a knight watching some event unfolding before his eyes. As spectator and knight in one person, he sees Christ being laid in the tomb. The painting was conventional in style (like those of Titorelli), but quite recent. If ever our hearts are moved in this story, it is here. A kind of Gestalt in which the whole psyche moves with precision and beauty toward its fulfillment in death and rebirth has occurred in the incidental chapel to the side. The ultimate question in Kafka criticism is this: could Joseph K. have dreamed of the Resurrection morn?

But Joseph, with the ignorance of the dreamer, as dictated and demanded by his diseased ego, turns off the electric torch no wiser than he was before he saw it. Our hearts almost literally burn within us. We thought he might be saved. Though a soul fails to get born, aesthetically we are moved by the splendor of the truth, its consonance with every other lost chance—or chance at inward knowledge given by a gracious unconscious to a corrupted ego. It is pathetic; it is awful; it is tragic in a casual, dreamlike way. For, after all, what is there to a dream? For the critics to talk at this point about the ecclesiastical cabala being satirized or exposed by Kafka shows the incredible stupidity of the critic who can't interpret the dream. This is Joseph K.'s consciousness flowing down as spectator into the perfectly religious unconscious.

Well, we go on with the rest of the tragic story. There is no communal faith manifest in the sacrifice of the mass and the communicants' repeating the eternal reconciliation of the particular and the universal in the union of God and man in Christ. It is Joseph K. alone who comes into colloquy with the last paternal imago his unconscious can create—the prison chaplain. This is the voice without the law, not the voice from within the door to the law. Joseph hasn't entered; he is the man from the country. He has been accused; the case is going badly; the unconscious makes a supreme effort to speak by parable; this is the father-imago as preceptor and prophet. In the cleanest moment of the ego's life, relations between the absolute and the ego are almost friendly, and again we wait breathlessly to see what will happen.

Nothing happens. A single effort is made to look past the censor that Joseph K. has created. He is intimidated by the fears deposited in the censor, or doorkeeper. The most ridiculous vestige of the infantile father-fantasy enters the construct. The doorkeeper is a Tartar, with a long nose and, of all things, vermin in his collar. This is, of course, the resurgence, at the most crucial point of all, of the decomposed image of the father—the imago, or fantasy, of the father as one who threatens dire punishments to the boy who wants to know where babies come from, who has only the crude fantasies of the scene in the studio with Titorelli, the unconscious image-maker and painter of things in true, classical, archetypal style. The father who withholds knowledge is the Hermann Kafka known in fantasy to little Franz Kafka. So, Joseph K. sits down and waits before the construct manufactured by the little boy's frustrated quest for forbidden knowledge and waits until he dies—even though he is now in the very prime of life. For a whole year has this case been going on, and Joseph K. is now thirty-one years old, the same age as Kafka himself. Can you believe it? Well, it is so. He begs, he prays, naturally, to the vermin he has projected into this ambivalent image of the father; he bribes, and his bribes are accepted. But having failed to reconstruct a father who welcomes masculinity in the son, he can return only to the home he has made for his particular father in his own unconscious. To what a different home did that other prodigal son return when he came to himself and moved in action toward a reconciliation of the past and the present. His youthful sins in the unconscious were discharged in the forward thrust of a living soul.

But not so with Joseph K. He resorts, as usual, to endless dispute. He wants to know without accepting the risk of action. And he learns that "the right perception of any matter and a misunderstanding of the same matter do not wholly exclude each other." This is the vice in the intellect of the defense mechanism known as "isolation." It is characteristically true of scientists and English professors. The harassed ego abstracts all feeling-tones or affects and rationalizes until every possibility but the right one has been considered. And so, in the next scene, "The End," the court, having rendered its decision, the procedures having quietly drawn to a close, Joseph K. is led to castration and death. His logic was infallible. And the logic of the unconscious is absolute. "As a man thinketh in his heart [or unconscious], so is he." Surely this, the second of Kafka's major works, is the most perfect expressionistic writing in the world today.

A word of explanation—since the interpretation follows the dream. In formulating the fantasy-father, the five-year-old Franz Kafka recreated the ancient wrong and held his father guilty of destroying his personality for the rest of his life. Fixated on this infantile level of libido, he sought release in genitalized form only to be thrown back on his own narcissism and the terror of homosexuality. Experimental sexual relations in puberty found him constantly defeated from within, the victim of the fantasy-father who castrates. To guard himself from the disease within, he identifies himself exclusively with the ego and strives to escape from the father-fantasy within and the real father in the home. *Amerika* (1912) is a projection of the geographical escape and the movement, within, through the perils of masochism before the male to the Oklahoma theater where he is accepted as a person. He strives in the social ego to obtain maturity. *The Trial* (1914) records his arrest at the age of thirty by an invasion from the distressed and dammed-up libido in the unconscious. The infantile fantasy is worked out, with the logic of the unconscious, and its power, prevailing. He moves on in *The Castle* (1922) toward the further quest of the unconscious, resolves some aspects of the cultural dilemmas in fantasy—in general toward greater understanding and acquiescence in the role of the unconscious. Recently, additional chapters have been published giving greater cohesion to the unfinished work. At thirty-two, Kafka left his father's home; at thirty-six, he wrote the hundred-page "Letter to My Father," his apologia pro vita sua, never delivered by his mother and still published only in part. With Dora Dymant he knew a brief season of love, as he fought the ravages of the tuberculosis he claimed to have chosen as a way out of marriage. His short life (1883-1924) is told in moving form by Brod, but these novels, and short stories and tales like "The Metamorphosis," "In the Penal Colony," and "The Burrow," reveal still better the reality within a psyche destroying itself by hatred for the father displaced upon itself. He is a magnificent writer. He is perfectly honest except for that statistical criminal within, which denied the reality of the voice from within the law itself.

Erwin R. Steinberg

K. of The Castle: *Ostensible Land-Surveyor*

Most critics seem to take at its face value K.'s statement at the beginning of *The Castle* that he is a land-surveyor hired by the Count. Ronald Gray, for example, says, "K. at once affects, on his arrival at the inn, to have no inkling of the castle's presence, though it soon becomes obvious that he has come because of a summons from the owner of the castle himself."[1]

Tauber does indicate at first that K. is not what he seems: "K. pretends that he has been appointed by the Castle as Land Surveyor. ..."[2] But he never examines the implications of that pretense, and immediately after his announcement of it writes as though K.'s claim was valid. A few lines later, for example, he calls K. "The Land Surveyor" (p. 133). And a few pages later he indicates that he considers that at least after K. arrives he has a valid appointment—although it "is valid only in an equivocal way, so that the appointed man is at the same time not appointed" (p. 136). And he goes on to speak of "the history of his appointment" and the "acts of carelessness [which] played a part in his appointment" (p. 136).

Whether K. is in fact what he claims to be is an important point which should be examined carefully. For if K.'s seeking to be accepted by the Castle is symbolic of man's seeking salvation, questioning the

[1] Ronald Gray, *Kafka's Castle* (Cambridge, England: Cambridge University Press, 1956), p. 27.
[2] Herbert Tauber, *Franz Kafka* (London: Martin Secker and Warburg, Ltd., 1948), p. 132.

From College English *(December 1965), Vol. 27, No. 3, pp. 185-189. Copyright © 1965 by the National Council of Teachers of English. Reprinted by permission of the publisher and the author.*

validity of K.'s credentials and thus his right to press his claim on the Castle raises the parallel question of man's right to salvation.

An examination of *The Castle* indicates that there is little evidence to support K.'s claim either that he is a land-surveyor or that he was hired by the Castle. And there is a good bit of evidence to the contrary. Let us look first at the opening scene in which he makes his claim. Questioned about his presence, K. replies:

> "What village is this I have wandered into? Is there a castle here?"
>
> "Most certainly," replied the young man slowly, while here and there a head was shaken over K.'s remark, "the castle of my lord the Count Westwest."[3]

K. admits that he *wandered into* the village. He obviously does not know where he is. There is nothing about the statement that suggests a purposeful visit. Nor is there anything to suggest, as Gray says, that "K. ... affects to have no inkling of the castle's presence." The only reason to question the honesty of K.'s indication that he knows nothing about a castle lies in his claim made immediately after, that he has been hired by the Count. But as we shall see, that claim itself is highly questionable.

Pressed by the ill-mannered Schwarzer, K. strikes back:

> "Enough of this fooling," said K. in a markedly quiet voice, laying himself down again and pulling up the blanket. "You're going a little too far, my good fellow, and I'll have something to say tomorrow about your conduct. ... Let me tell you that I am the Land-Surveyor whom the Count is expecting. My assistants are coming on tomorrow in a carriage with the apparatus. ... That it was too late to present myself at the Castle I knew very well before you saw fit to inform me. That is why I have made shift with this bed for the night, where, to put it mildly, you have had the discourtesy to disturb me. That is all I have to say. Good night, gentlemen." And K. turned over on his side toward the stove. (p. 5)

Schwarzer's call to the Castle brings a quick denial of K.'s claim. But almost immediately a call from the Castle brings a reversal of that denial. K.'s claim, it would seem, is genuine (p. 7).

Later, however, we are warned against trusting any message that comes from the Castle over the phone. In talking with K., the mayor says:

[3] Franz Kafka, *The Castle* (definitive edition), (New York, 1959), p. 4.

When anybody calls up the Castle from here, the instruments in all the subordinate departments ring, or rather they would all ring if practically all the departments—I know for a certainty—didn't leave their receivers off. Now and then, however, a fatigued official may feel the need of a little distraction, especially in the evenings and at night, and may hang the receiver up. Then we get an answer, but an answer of course that's merely a practical joke. And that's very understandable too. For who would take the responsibility of interrupting, in the middle of the night, the extremely important work up there that goes on furiously the whole time, with a message about his own little private troubles? I can't understand how even a stranger can imagine that when he calls up Sordini, for example, it's really Sordini that answers. Far more probably it's a little copying clerk from an entirely different department. On the other hand, it may certainly happen once in a blue moon that when one calls up the little copying clerk Sordini himself will answer. Then, indeed, the best thing is to fly from the telephone before the first sound comes through. (p. 94)

In the light of such a statement, the curious reversal of the Castle's original denial of K.'s claim becomes highly suspicious.

Furthermore, K.'s reaction to the Castle's acceptance of his claim raises doubts:

K. pricked up his ears. So the Castle had recognized him as the Land-Surveyor. That was unpropitious for him, on the one hand, for it meant that the Castle was well informed about him, had estimated all the probable chances, and was taking up the challenge with a smile. On the other hand, however, it was quite propitious, for if his interpretation was right they had underestimated his strength, and he would have more freedom of action than he had dared to hope. And if they expected to cow him by their lofty superiority in recognizing him as Land-Surveyor, they were mistaken; it made his skin prickle a little, that was all. (pp. 7-8)

If K. really is a land-surveyor hired by the Castle, why is it "unpropitious for him" that the Castle had recognized him? What can the statement of the Castle's "taking up the challenge with a smile" mean other than that K.'s claim is a false one and that he is being dared to prove it? If he really is the land-surveyor, why should he take the Castle's recognition of him as a sign that the Castle was trying "to cow him"?

The matter of the Assistants is further evidence against K.'s claim. According to K.'s original statement, they are due the next day with his apparatus (p. 5). The next day, two men who purport to be his assistants do appear!

Not until he was up with the landlord, who greeted him humbly, did he notice two men, one on either side of the doorway. ... it was the men he had already met, who were called Arthur and Jeremiah. ... "Who are you?" he asked, looking from one to the other. "Your assistants," they answered. ... "What?" said K.; "are you my old assistants, whom I told to follow me and whom I am expecting?" They answered in the affirmative. "That's good," observed K. after a short pause; "I'm glad you've come. Well," he said after another pause, "you've come very late; you're very slack." "It was a long way to come," said one of them. "A long way?" repeated K.; "but I met you just now coming from the Castle." "Yes," said they without further explanation. "Where is the apparatus?" asked K. "We haven't any," said they. "The apparatus I gave you?" said K. "We haven't any," they reiterated. "Oh, you are fine fellows!" said K.; "do you know anything about surveying?" "No," said they. "But if you are my old assistants you must know something about it," said K. They made no reply. "Well, come in," said K., pushing them before him into the house. (pp. 23-24)

It is obvious from the passage that Arthur and Jeremiah are not K.'s assistants. Later evidence proves them to have been sent by the Castle (p. 302).

The scene also suggests that K. is not expecting assistants. For surely if he is he would not take Arthur and Jeremiah. For if he does, when his own assistants appear, how could he explain to the already suspicious villagers his acceptance of the two from the Castle? Surely a surveyor can be expected to know his own assistants. The obvious answer is that the statement about assistants is as untrue as the statement that K. is a land-surveyor.

There is other evidence of the same kind throughout the book. A curious letter arrives acknowledging that K. has been "engaged for the Count's service" (p. 30). But it says nothing about surveying; and as K. himself notices, it uses terms which suggest a much lesser status:

There was of course a danger, and that was sufficiently emphasized in the letter, even elaborated with a certain satisfaction, as if it were unavoidable. That was sinking to the workman's level—"service," "superior," "work," "terms of employment," "responsible," "workers,"—the letter fairly reeked of it, and even though more personal messages were included, they were written from the standpoint of an employer. (p.32)

The summary of K.'s thoughts about the letter denies K.'s original claim of having been invited to the village by the Count:

Nor did the letter pass over the fact that if it should come to a struggle, K. had had the hardihood to make the first advances; it was very subtly indicated and only to be sensed by an uneasy conscience—an uneasy conscience, not a bad one. It lay in the three words "as you know," referring to his engagement in the Count's service. K. had reported his arrival, and only after that, as the letter pointed out, had he known that he was engaged. (p. 33)

Later, the Mayor indicates that the village has no need of a surveyor (p. 77). And when the landlady charges K. with having lied about his claim ("You're not telling the truth. Why don't you tell the truth?"), he does not press his claim or become indignant at the charge. He simply replies, "You don't tell the truth either" (p. 411).

The clearest evidence, however, that K.'s claim of having been hired by the Castle as the land-surveyor is false comes in the fourteenth chapter, where a summary of K.'s thoughts indicates very clearly that he came to the village "as a wandering stranger" who expected to leave the next day, or perhaps a day or two later at the most in the unlikely event that he found some work:

> Because of Schwarzer the full attention of the authorities had been most unreasonably directed to K. at the very first hour of his arrival, while he was still a complete stranger in the village, without a single acquaintance or an alternative shelter; overtired with walking as he was and quite helpless on his sack of straw, he had been at the mercy of any official action. One night later might have made all the difference, things might have gone quietly and been only half noticed. At any rate nobody would have known anything about him or have had any suspicions, there would have been no hesitation in accepting him at least for one day as a stray wanderer, his handiness and trustworthiness would have been recognized and spoken of in the neighborhood, and probably he would soon have found accommodation somewhere as a servant. Of course the authorities would have found him out. But there would have been a big difference between having the Central Bureau, or whoever was on the telephone, disturbed on his account in the middle of the night by an insistent though ostensibly humble request for an immediate decision, made, too, by Schwarzer, who was probably not in the best odor up there, and a quiet visit by K. to the Mayor on the next day during official hours to report himself in proper form as a wandering stranger who had already found quarters in a respectable house, and who would probably be leaving the place tomorrow unless the unlikely were to happen and he found some work in the village, only for a day or two, of course, since he did not mean to stay longer. (p. 216)

Certainly these are not the thoughts of a man who had been invited to the village by the local authorities to serve as its surveyor.

The Publisher's introductory Note to the definitive edition of the novel (and as indicated, in earlier editions the Editor's Note) carries a warning that K.'s claim is not to be trusted:

> As The Castle remains unfinished, however, the following paragraph from the Editor's Note to the first American edition should be preserved: "Kafka never wrote his concluding chapter. But he told me about it once when I asked him how the novel was to end. The ostensible Land-Surveyor was to find partial satisfaction at least. He was not to relax in his struggle, but was to die worn out by it. Round his deathbed the villagers were to assemble, and from the Castle itself the word was to come that though K.'s legal claim to live in the village was not valid, yet, taking certain auxiliary circumstances into account, he was to be permitted to live and work there." (p. vi)

The important point is not that the Castle branded K.'s legal claim "not valid," but rather that Max Brod—and perhaps even Kafka himself—referred to K. as the "*ostensible* Land-Surveyor." If the adjective could be proven to have been Kafka's, the case against K.'s claim could be declared, perhaps, a little stronger. It rests securely enough, however, on the textual evidence given above.

This demonstration of the lack of validity to K.'s claim adds an additional dimension to the usual interpretation of *The Castle*. Critics generally interpret the novel as the story of man's attempt to reach salvation, religious, or otherwise. Thomas Mann, for example, in his introductory "Homage" to the novel describes "K.'s relations with the 'Castle,' or rather [his attempt] to set up relations with it [as an attempt] to attain nearer, in other words, to God and to a state of grace" (p. xiv). Tauber understands the novel to mean that: "The striving after justice, after the unequivocal word is in vain. But it is also not publicly refuted, because in it a basis of truth is effective: man's being coordinate with a spiritual certainty, with a real significance of his personal existence with God" (pp. 183-184). Camus speaks of K.'s "attempt . . . to recapture God [and] to try to enter . . . the desert of divine grace."[4]

It is one thing, however, for a man—or Man—to seek a salvation to which he feels he has some right. In many religions, for example, the possibility of that right is explicit: it may either be given by election or

---

[4] Albert Camus, "Hope and the Absurd in the Work of Franz Kafka," in *The Myth of Sisyphus* (New York, 1960), p. 99.

earned by prayer, acts of penitence, or good works. In *The Castle*, if K. is indeed a land-surveyor and if he has indeed been hired by the Count, he has some reason (or right) to expect to get through to the Castle, to communicate with the Count or his emissaries. And symbolically, if a man—or Man—has been chosen or has earned consideration from God, he has a reason (or a right) to expect salvation.

But how if, as I have attempted to show above, K.'s claim is false? Then he is making demands he has no right to make. He is seeking a salvation he has neither been awarded nor has earned.

If this is the picture that Kafka is giving us, then to the previous interpretations of *The Castle* we must add an additional ironic twist. Not only does K. pursue doggedly a salvation he cannot hope to achieve (or, if one credits Brod's story about the conclusion Kafka planned for the novel, he receives too late—p. vi). He seeks a salvation which he has not been promised, which he has not earned, and to which he has no reason to feel he has a right. If this is Kafka's picture of Man's journey through life or of his relation to God, it is even more bitter than critics in the past have led us to believe. Not only will Man not achieve salvation. He is presumptuous in even seeking it.

Klaus Mann

Preface to Amerika

In [Kafka's] lifetime only a dozen initiated friends and connoisseurs grasped the puzzling phenomenon of his greatness. Only those selected few realized the philosophic and artistic significance of his short prose compositions and his three fragmentary novels, *The Castle, The Trial,* and *Amerika*—forming in their entity a sublime "trilogy of human solitude," to use a formula of the novelist and critic Max Brod. To the rank and file of *literati,* Kafka was just another curious character whom one met occasionally at a café—a sickly youth of an aristocratic Jewish type: melancholy, shy, gifted with an almost frightening seriousness and a bizarre sense of humor. He was no bohemian . . . rather pedantic in the tidiness of his appearance; unpresuming, amiable and reserved; sometimes enchanting by the natural gracefulness of his manners—sometimes disquieting through the profound sadness of his eye and smile. He always looked younger than he really was. Even a picture taken in the last year of his fatal disease—in 1924—shows a juvenile figure—slightly stooping but elastic and elegant. He was forty-one when he died. At that time most of his works were still unpublished.

It was partly his mysterious pride, partly his genuine modesty that made him averse to any kind of publicity. His friends had to struggle with him for a manuscript they wanted to send to a literary magazine or a publishing-house. He left no will—except the strict injunction that all of his posthumous papers should be burned. His nearest, most trusted and understanding friend, Max Brod, had to meet the agonizing dilemma. Should he neglect Kafka's imperious and cruel wish? Was he to destroy a literary treasure the singularity of which he fully recognized?

The decision he finally made—to save and edit the manuscripts—was, of course, the only right and honorable one. It is to him, to Max Brod, that we actually owe the preservation of Kafka's work; he is chiefly responsible for the gradual, belated growing of Kafka's fame.

May we speak of "fame" in the peculiar case of an author who neither sought nor gained popularity and never was "a success" in the ordinary sense of the word? Kafka's books were not best-sellers—not even in pre-Nazi Germany, so impressionable and eagerly open to all kinds of artistic experiments. Yet the actual effect of his works has been more intense and lasting than that of many a literary sensation of the day: his subterranean influence has proven penetrating and mysteriously strong. One critic has called him "the secret king of modern German prose." But awareness of this inconspicuous greatness gradually crossed the boundaries of the German-speaking world. Most of his writings were translated into many languages; essays on Kafka were written, not only in German but also in English and French, Spanish, Czech, Swedish and Hungarian. His personal style—that unmistakable compound of baroque and classic elements, of dreamlike romanticism and realistic exactness— has inspired and influenced young writers on both sides of the Atlantic.

"What we call Fame is nothing but the sum of all mistakes circulating about one individual." These words, haughty and resigned, are Rainer Maria Rilke's—another genius whose princely shyness despised and banished the clamorous approach of mass curiosity. Even Kafka, for all his aristocratic reserves, was not spared awkward misinterpretations. He has been identified with the Surrealists, and with a certain decadent Viennese school: there were even attempts at analyzing from a Marxist angle certain enigmatic passages in his books. All such interpretations are, of course, erroneous, and utterly fail to define the true substance of his being and writing.

He never meant to surprise and startle his readers by macabre tricks. He wanted to be plastic, plain and simple. His literary masters were Flaubert and Tolstoi rather than Baudelaire and Dostoievski. He has been compared with Edgar Allan Poe, but he admired Dickens. His supreme ambition was to describe the dismay and ecstasy of his inward adventures as thoroughly and realistically as Flaubert described all the details of Madame Bovary's appearance, or Tolstoi the face and smell of a Russian peasant. Kafka is no surrealist but the most realistic explorer of spheres that are not less real for their being inaccessible to average travelers. His topography of nightmare landscapes is as precise as any scientific report.

The humorous, grotesque element in his descriptions—disturbing to some of his admirers, and overestimated by others—is nothing but the natural consequence of his sober honesty. His own experiences taught him that even the Mystery has comic aspects—aspects well known, by the way, to medieval saints and sculptors. The Devil, or at least his minor emissaries, can assume a very clownish appearance—funny as well as fiendish. There are Gothic statues in which we recognize that horrified laughter characteristic of Kafka's sinister wit. What inconceivable tribulation must have frozen his tears, numbed the outcry of his despair, and left him that lurid jocularity as his only solace!

Kafka was haunted by all sorts of fears and apprehensions. Ideas of Original Sin, of Guilt and Punishment were the very basis of his feeling and thinking. The God to whom he sent his almost hopeless prayers and whose Holy name he hardly ever mentioned, is Jehova, the Lord of Revenge, and there is no Savior to reconcile doomed mortal creatures with their merciless Father. Human beings have constantly to atone for crimes the gravity and even the names of which they cannot know. Our mysterious guilt is examined in an eternal trial; there is a hierarchy of hidden judges—and even the lowest is of such overwhelming majesty that we could not bear to see him face to face.

These fixed ideas and creative torments are deeply rooted, of course, in many circumstances and experiences of Kafka's personal life. The autobiographic content of his narratives is stronger than it may seem at first. Any psychoanalyst could define Kafka's religious pathos—his humble and yet mistrustful fear of God—as the productive "sublimation" of an obvious "father complex." The patriarchal figure of his father played, indeed, a predominant role in Kafka's biography. He admired and dreaded the father because of his solid strength, his well-balanced vitality. The father was the one who had lived as a man *should* live—who had mastered life: whereas the son, for all the problematic rapture of his inspiration, considered himself a failure in all matters that really count.

A failure he was, indeed, as far as crude realities of life are concerned: he could not stand the work in a gloomy office; he had no spectacular success as an author, never made enough money to support himself; his poor health prevented him from marrying: the one great romance of his life was doomed to dreary frustration.

He suffered—not only from his disease, but from life itself—life as a Jew, in Prague, in the tumultuous period of World War and Revolution. He was scarcely interested in politics. Social problems appear in his books only indirectly—disguised, transposed into a remote and mysterious sphere. His vision of *The Trial* and *The Castle,* in which the invisible Power hides, was influenced, not only by the esoteric wisdom of the Cabala, but also by his own experiences as a minor functionary of the ancient Austrian Bureaucracy. His vast and meticulous epic of a capricious tyranny has no seditious verve nor is it really satirical. Kafka's attitude toward the worldly authorities expresses the same half-ironic apprehension and critical respect characteristic of his devotion to the inscrutable Father, human or divine.

The city of Prague meant to him, in a weird and definite way, the microcosm in which he recognized the tragedy and struggle of mankind. Prague was actually *all he knew*—his entire world, his paradise and his prison. He yearned for other landscapes, for a lighter and brighter beauty. But the few journeys he could afford, in the company of friends or alone, were short and hardly satisfactory.

The most extensive journey he ever made took place wholly in his mind. The goal of his bold excursion was the United States. His friends were highly surprised when he confided to them his secret—that he was going to write a novel entitled *Amerika:* in fact, he had already begun.

"What do you know about America?" they asked. And he answered, cheerfully: "I know the autobiography of Benjamin Franklin, and I always admired Walt Whitman, and I like the Americans because they are healthy and optimistic." He imagined that all Americans wore a perpetual smile. Later, in the years of his fatal disease, he met in a sanatorium several Americans who quite often grumbled and complained. He was deeply disappointed. But when he conceived his novel *Amerika,* in 1913, he knew no Americans at all and understood very little English. His only sources of information were the few books he had read—and his own poetic imagination.

He seemed unusually cheerful and confident while working on *Amerika.* His friends were pleased to notice that his looks and mood had improved almost miraculously. His relative optimism, however, did not entirely protect him from qualms and scruples. He was at that time reading, or re-reading, several novels by Dickens, and made the following remarks in his diary:

"Dickens, *Copperfield.* 'The Stoker,' a plain imitation of Dickens: even more so than the planned novel." (The first chapter of the America novel was published as a special little volume, called 'The Stoker,' before the novel appeared.) . . . My intention was, as I now see, to write a Dickens novel, enriched by the sharper lights which I took from our modern times, and by the pallid ones I would have found in my own interior—Dickens' wealth and naive, sweeping power: but, consequently, moments of horrible weakness. . . . The impression of the senseless whole is barbaric—a barbarism which I was able to avoid thanks to my decadence. . . ."

Strangely enough, in Kafka's mind the figure and the works of Dickens were vitally connected with the American atmosphere and landscape. It was not Dickens' biting satire on America, in *Martin Chuzzlewit,* that lay behind this odd identification. The picture that Kafka cherished was of a fatherly genius called Charles Dickens being welcomed to New York with wild enthusiasm by thousands of his American readers. Kafka often described to his friends the hilarious spectacle of all that exuberant public jammed on the dock, eagerly awaiting a new chapter of *David Copperfield*, waving and shouting as the boat with its literary treasure slowly pulls in.

As to his own novel, *Amerika*, he was far from accurate when he called it an "imitation of Dickens." For the resemblance to Dickens is only accidental and superficial—while the differences between the sentimental or humorous circumstantiality of Dickens' style and Kafka's visionary precision are basic and essential.

The adolescent heroes of the English master-novelist have to endure suffering and adventures because the world is wicked—and because the great narrator had to offer an exciting plot. But Karl Rossmann, the leading character of Kafka's story, is harassed by more profound and complicated dangers: the problem of guilt *as such,* the mystic curse of Original Sin follows him over the ocean. We see this naive but observant lad as he arrives in New York, welcomed by "the free breezes" of America and a Statue of Liberty furnished most surprisingly (and perhaps symbolically?), with an upraised sword. He seems almost happy, in spite of the hardships ahead—happy, at least, as compared with his tragic relatives, the doomed heroes of Kafka's two other novels, *The Castle* and *The Trial.* Both of these remain strangely anonymous—or rather, they hide their mysterious identity with the author behind the obvious initial "K"; while young Karl Rossmann is permitted a name of his own, in which the fatal "K" appears, but does not predominate. He is a younger, more fortunate brother of that nameless being, K., for whom there will be no America: the one who must remain in Europe, in Prague, to endure the merciless decisions of the inscrutable judges.

It may be, however, that Karl is guilty as well—notwithstanding the maid-servant's confession that she was the active party in the sordid affair that precipitated the youth's departure from Europe. He is not responsible—according to human judgment. But our judgment is, of course, subject to error and is easily refuted by the sentence of the higher authorities.

What is our guilt? Who defines its roots, its consequences, and the chastisement it may deserve? Nobody knows if the stoker, that pathetic hero of the introductory chapter, is innocent or guilty—and the wayward laws dominating Karl Rossmann's life are not less mysterious. At first he seems favored by a playful fate as he meets, almost miraculously, his benign and wealthy uncle, a certain Senator Jacob. But the uncle repudiates him as surprisingly as he offered him his protection—and we

find the young adventurer, abandoned by his mighty benefactor, penni-
less and friendless on the highways, in a vast and unknown country.
What an amazing panorama!—this American landscape seen through
the clairvoyant eyes of a naive and sensitive youth. Every detail of
Kafka's description of American life is quite inaccurate, and yet the
picture as a whole has poetical truth. The hyper-modern desk which the
generous uncle puts at his nephew's disposal looks like a grotesque piece
of furniture in a Charlie Chaplin film; it is an alarming object with innumerable technical tricks—secret drawers that pop open when one
touches a hidden button, little trapdoors, complicated locks. The country house of a millionaire near New York is built like an ancient European
castle—a typical Kafka castle in fact—confusing, frightening, with countless corridors and galleries, tremendous staircases and an unfinished
chapel. And those astounding streets of American cities, with the Gothic
lines of steel-constructed skyscrapers profiled against a wan, colorless
sky, like cathedrals from another planet where people are praying to
another God! Those endless highways, flanked by little inns and dusty
gardens where dirty men hastily swallow indescribable liquids and
waiters run around with distorted faces as if in permanent pain.

Yet, in the midst of this bewitched scenery, the great Trial
continues—that tremendous drama of Justice which is also a farce—full
of a sardonic irony; puzzling, terrifying and funny. Friendly and evil
ghosts seem to fight with each other for the possession of Karl's soul,
just as God and the Devil dispute for Doctor Faust in the medieval
miracle-play. And a miracle-play it is, comic and profound, in which
Karl acts as hero, victim, sinner, martyr and clown. The benign *Ober-
köchin*, the Supreme Cook in the Hotel Occidental, represents the principle of Good. But even this efficient guardian angel proves incapable of
helping her protegé when he finds himself in an alarming mess brought
about by two fiendish demons, Delamarche and Robinson, who keep
tagging behind the child-like wanderer. The grand and appalling chapter,
describing Karl's humiliation as a servant of these two ghastly crooks and
their prodigious mistress, represents the burlesque and moving climax of
the adventurous story.

But as though the author found it intolerable to continue this
macabre report, he suddenly breaks off his narrative, and when Karl
re-appears—months, perhaps years later—he is looking for a new job, and
finds one in *The Great Nature Theater of Oklahoma*—a kind of gigantic
WPA project,* organized and financed by invisible but extremely powerful benefactors. Kafka was especially fond of this concluding chapter,
and his friends tell us that he used to read it aloud in an "unforgettable
manner." With an enigmatic smile he declared that his young hero, Karl
Rossmann, might well find again, "in this almost boundless theater,"

---

*The WPA was a public-works program undertaken by the federal government
to alleviate unemployment during the great depression of the 1930s.

his profession, his security and freedom, and perhaps even his homeland and parents—"as by a celestial spell."

Kafka himself was not in a position to describe these happy developments. The novel had to remain a fragment as did all of his greater compositions, according to their imperative inherent law. The very themes of these works—the topics of Guilt and Atonement, human loneliness and the unfathomable riddle of the Supreme Law—prohibit them from finding an end; they are essentially and necessarily *endless.* *Amerika,* however, is the only one of Kafka's fragmentary novels on the last pages of which a confident mood prevails. The youthful hero disappears—running, capering like a reckless foal in the midst of a vast, heroic landscape. His tragic brother and creator, Franz Kafka, watches the agile figure gradually shrinking between the hugh hills, trees and buildings. Finally the poet turns away his beautiful, shadowed forehead, bidding a plaintive farewell of mingled tenderness and renunciation.

Kafka's excursion to the New World has come to an end. Here they are again—the gloomy streets of Prague, the familiar background of his suffering. The city, numb and solemn, welcomes her prodigal son. The baroque statues, the cathedrals, the mysterious dwellings of the alchemists, the libraries, the strange and sweetish smells of the ghetto—all this well-known beauty, well-known horror, receive him with a faint, unfathomable smile: Here you are—our son, our prisoner, our poet; this is Europe—your chain, your curse and your love: Europe, your bitter love: you must bear it, accept it. *Here,* you must continue your writing, your meditations and prayers; seeking and fearing God. *Here* you must bear the torments of your religious persecution mania, and must transform your constant agonies into the brittle beauty of your lucid prose. Here, you must serve and perish, to earn at last the gloomy crown—the dark glory of your own destruction. Bow your head! Recognize your fate! There is no escape.

He accepts his lot. He is brave—the delicate but tenacious son of an ancient, heroic race, most experienced in suffering, humiliation, and long endurance. But sometimes, surely, his loving, sorrowful thoughts must have wandered over the ocean, to visit that errant youth whom he had created and abandoned there. To him he sends his wishes and his hopes. He wants Karl to be courageous—as courageous, indeed, as in his own place his elder brother—"K"—is obliged to be. The poet and prophet must glorify and analyze his doom; must continue his dialogue with a hidden God—indefatigable, witty, passionate, desperate, and yet faithful. But Karl has to *live*—no easy task either. And he must live in America. He has, therefore, a special chance. His creator hopes that he may prove worthy of it. He does not want him to perish. For the poet, in all his glory and misery, deeply and simply loves his innocent creature, his favorite dream, his heir.

Roland Barthes

Kafka's Answer

> In the duel between you and the world, back
> the world. — Franz Kafka

A moment has passed, the moment of committed literature. The end of the Sartrean novel, the imperturbable indigence of socialist fiction, the defects of political theater—all that, like a receding wave, leaves exposed a singular and singularly resistant object: literature. Already, moreover, an opposing wave washes over it, the wave of an asserted detachment: revival of the love story, hostility to "ideas," cult of fine writing, refusal to be concerned with the world's significations: a whole new ethic of art is being proposed, consisting of a convenient swivel between romanticism and off-handedness, between the (minimal) risks of poetry and the (effective) protection of intelligence.

Is our literature forever doomed to this exhausting oscillation between political realism and art-for-art's-sake, between an ethic of commitment and an esthetic purism, between compromise and asepsis? Must it always be poor (if it is merely itself) or embarrassed (if it is anything but itself)? Can it not have a proper place in *this world*?

This question now receives an exact answer: Marthe Robert's *Kafka*. Is it Kafka who answers? Yes, of course (for it is hard to imagine a more scrupulous exegesis than this one), but we must make no mistake: Kafka is not Kafka-ism. For twenty years, Kafka-ism has nourished the most contrary literatures, from Camus to Ionesco. If we are concerned with describing the bureaucratic terror of the modern moment, *The Trial, The Castle, The Penal Colony* constitute over-

Reprinted from Roland Barthes, Critical Essays, *translated by Richard Howard (1966), by permission of Northwestern University Press, Evanston, Illinois.*

worked models. If we are concerned with exposing the claims of individualism against the invasion of objects, "The Metamorphosis" is a profitable gimmick. Both realistic and subjective, Kafka's *oeuvre* lends itself to everyone but answers no one. It is true that we do not question it much, for writing in the shadow of his themes does not constitute a question; as Marthe Robert says, solitude, alienation, the quest, the familiarity of the absurd, in short the constants of what is called the Kafkaesque universe—don't these belong to all our writers, once they refuse to write in the service of a world of ownership? As a matter of fact, Kafka's answer is addressed to the person who has questioned him least, to *the artist*.

This is what Marthe Robert tells us: that Kafka's meaning is in his *technique*. A brand new argument, not only in relation to Kafka, but in relation to all our literature, so that Marthe Robert's apparently modest commentary (is this not one more book on Kafka, published in a pleasant popularizing series?) forms a profoundly original essay, providing that good, that precious nourishment of the mind which results from the correspondence of an intelligence and an interrogation.

For after all, paradoxical as it seems, we possess virtually nothing on literary technique. When a writer reflects on his art (something for the most part rare and abhorred), it is to tell us how he conceives the world, what relations he entertains with it, his image of Man; in short, each writer says he is a realist, never how. Now literature is only a means, devoid of cause and purpose; in fact, that is what defines it. You can of course attempt a sociology of the literary institution; but you can limit the act of writing by neither a *why* nor a *wherefore*. The writer is like the artisan who diligently fabricates some complicated object, as ignorant of its model as of its use, analogous to Ashby's homeostat. To ask oneself why one writes is already an advance over the blissful unconsciousness of "inspiration," but it is a despairing advance—there is no answer. Apart from demand and apart from success, empirical alibis much more than real motives, the literary act is without cause and without goal precisely because it is devoid of sanction: it proposes itself to the world without any *praxis* establishing or justifying it: it is an absolutely intransitive act, it modifies nothing, nothing *reassures* it.

So then? Well, that is its paradox; this act exhausts itself in its technique, it exists only in the condition of a manner. For the (sterile) old question: *why write*? Marthe Robert's *Kafka* substitutes a new question: *how write*? And this *how* exhausts the *why*: all at once the impasse is cleared, a truth appears. This is Kafka's truth, this is Kafka's answer (to all those who want to write): *the being of literature is nothing but its technique*.

In short, if we transcribe this truth into semantic terms, this means that a work's specialty is not a matter of its concealed *signified* (no more criticism of "sources" and "ideas"), but only a matter of its *significations*. Kafka's truth is not Kafka's world (no more Kafka-ism), but the *signs* of that world. Thus the work is never an answer to the world's mystery; literature is never dogmatic. By imitating the world and its legends (Marthe Robert is right to devote a chapter of her essay to *imitation*, a crucial function of all great literature), the writer can show only the *sign* without the *signified*: the world is a place endlessly open to signification but endlessly dissatisfied by it. For the writer, literature is that utterance which says until death: I shall not begin to live before I know the meaning of life.

But saying that literature is no more than an interrogation of the world matters only if we propose a technique of interrogation, since this interrogation must persist throughout an apparently assertive narrative. Marthe Robert shows that Kafka's narrative is not woven of symbols, as we have been told so often, but is the fruit of an entirely different technique, the technique of allusion. All Kafka is in the difference. The symbol (Christianity's cross, for instance) is a *convinced* sign, it affirms a (partial) analogy between a form and an idea, it implies a certitude. If the figures and events of Kafka's narrative were symbolic, they would refer to a positive (even if it were a despairing) philosophy, to a universal Man: we cannot differ as to the meaning of a symbol, or else the symbol is a failure. Now, Kafka's narrative authorizes a thousand equally plausible keys—which is to say, it validates none.

Allusion is another matter altogether. It refers the fictive event to something besides itself, but to what? Allusion is a defective force, it undoes the analogy as soon as it has posited it. K is arrested on the orders of a tribunal: that is a familiar image of justice. But we learn that this tribunal does not regard crimes as our justice does: the resemblance is delusive, though not effaced. In short, as Marthe Robert explains, everything proceeds from a kind of semantic contraction: K feels he has been arrested, and everything happens *as if* K were really arrested (*The Trial*); Kafka's father treats him as a parasite, and everything happens *as if* Kafka were transformed into a parasite ("The Metamorphosis"). Kafka creates his work by systematically suppressing the *as ifs*: but it is the internal event which becomes the obscure term of the allusion.

Thus allusion, which is a pure technique of signification, is actually a commitment to the world, since it expresses the relation of an individual man and a common language: a system (abhorred phantom of every anti-intellectualism) produces one of the most fiery literatures which has ever existed. For example, Marthe Robert reminds us, we have commonplaces such as *like a dog, a dog's life, a Jew dog*; it suffices to make the metaphoric term the entire object of the narrative, shifting subjectivity to the allusive realm, in order for the insulted man to become a dog in fact: a man treated like a dog *is* a dog. Kafka's technique implies first of all an agreement with the world, a submission to ordinary language, but immediately afterwards, a reservation, a doubt, a fear before the letter of the signs the world proposes. As Marthe Robert puts it, Kafka's relations with the world are governed by a perpetual *yes, but* . . . One can fairly say as much of all our modern literature (and it is in this that Kafka has truly created it), since it identifies, in an inimitable fashion, the realistic project (*yes* to the world) and the ethical project (*but* . . .).

The trajectory separating the *yes* from the *but* is the whole uncertainty of signs, and it is because signs are uncertain that there is a literature. Kafka's technique says that the world's meaning is unutterable, that the artist's only task is to explore possible significations, each of which taken by itself will be only a (necessary) lie but whose multiplicity will be the writer's truth itself. That is Kafka's paradox: art depends on truth, but truth, being indivisible, cannot know itself: to *tell* the truth is to lie. Thus the writer *is* the truth, and yet when he speaks he lies: a work's authority is never situated at the level of its esthetic, but only at the level of the moral experience which makes it an assumed lie; or rather, as Kafka says correcting Kierkegaard: *we arrive at the esthetic enjoyment of being only through a moral experience without pride*.

Kafka's allusive system functions as a kind of enormous sign to interrogate other signs. Now, the exercise of a signifying system (mathematics, to take an example quite remote from literature) has only one requirement, which will therefore be the esthetic requirement itself: rigor. Any lapse, any vagueness in the construction of the allusive system would produce, paradoxically, symbols—would substitute an assertive language for the essentially interrogative function of literature. This is also Kafka's answer to all our inquiries into the novel today: that it is finally the precision of his writing (a structural, not a rhetorical precision, of course: it is not a matter of "fine writing") which commits the writer to the world: not in one of his options, but in his very defection: it is because the world is not finished that literature is possible.

Selected Bibliography

PRINCIPAL TRANSLATIONS OF KAFKA'S WORKS (ENGLISH)

The Penal Colony. Stories and Short Pieces. Translated by Willa and Edwin Muir. New York: Schocken Books, 1948 (paperback edition, 1961). This volume contains not only the title story but also "The Judgment," "The Metamorphosis," "A Country Doctor," "A Hunger Artist," "The Bucket Rider," "A Report to an Academy," and "Josephine the Singer, or the Mouse Folk."

Amerika. Translated by Edwin Muir, preface by Klaus Mann, afterward by Max Brod. New York: New Directions, 1940 (Schocken Books, paperback edition, 1962).

The Trial. Definitive edition, translated by Willa and Edwin Muir. Revised, with additional materials translated by E. M. Butler. New York: Alfred Knopf, 1957.

The Castle. Definitive edition. Translated by Willa and Edwin Muir, with additional material translated by Eithne Wilkins and Ernst Kaiser, with an homage by Thomas Mann. New York: Alfred Knopf, 1954.

Selected Short Stories of Franz Kafka. Translated by Willa and Edwin Muir. Introduced by Philip Rahv. New York: The Modern Library, 1952. The contents are similar to *The Penal Colony*.

The Great Wall of China. Stories and Reflections. Translated by Willa and Edwin Muir. New York: Schocken Books, paperback edition, 1970. This volume contains, in addition to the title story, "Investigations of a Dog," "The Burrow," and "Aphorisms."

Description of a Struggle. Translated by Tania and James Stern. New York: Schocken Books, 1958.

Parables and Paradoxes. Bilingual, German and English. New York: Schocken Books, paperback edition, 1961. (The first edition was called *Parables* and published in 1947.)

Letter to His Father. Bilingual edition. Translated by Ernst Kaiser and Eithne Wilkins. New York: Schocken Books, paperback edition, 1966.

The Diaries of Franz Kafka, 1910-1913. Edited by Max Brod. Translated by Joseph Kresh. New York: Schocken Books, paperback edition, 1965 (first edition 1947).

The Diaries of Franz Kafka, 1914-1923. Edited by Max Brod. Translated by Martin Greenberg, with the cooperation of Hannah Arendt. New York: Schocken Books, paperback edition, 1965 (first edition 1949).

Letters to Milena. Edited by Willie Haas. Translated by Tania and James Stern. New York: Schocken Books, paperback edition, 1962 (first edition 1953).

Letters to Felice. Edited by Erich Heller and Jurgen Born. Translated by James Stern and Elizabeth Duckworth. New York: Schocken Books, 1973.

Complete Short Stories. Edited by Nahum Glatzer. New York: Schocken Books, 1972.

The Trial: a Dramatization Based on Franz Kafka's Novel by André Gide and Jean-Louis Barrault. Translated by Leon Katz. New York: Schocken Books, 1964.

BIBLIOGRAPHY OF CRITICISM

Around a man who published only a half-dozen stories and sketches in his own lifetime there has grown up an immense literature. To Rudolph Hemmerle's *Franz Kafka: Ein Bibliographie* (Munich, 1958), which already listed some 1,300 words of criticism and exegesis, one must add the valuable check-list of "Bibliography and Criticism" in *Franz Kafka Today*, the bibliography in Heinz Politzer's *Franz Kafka: Parable and Paradox,* and Harry Jarv's *Die Kafka-Literatur,* which fills close to 400 pages and shows that from one corner of the globe to the other there is hardly a major language or literary culture that is without Kafka translations or commentaries (Russian is the one notable exception). The reader should also consult Maurice Beebe and Naomi Christensen, "Criticism of Franz Kafka," *Modern French Studies,* VIII (1962), 80-100, and Ann Thornton Benson, "Franz Kafka: An American Bibliography," *Bulletin of Bibliography,* XXII (1958), 112-114.

An invaluable guide to the post-war decade of Kafka exegesis is H.S. Reiss' "Recent Kafka Criticism, 1944-1953" in *German Life and Letters,* edited by James Boyd, Leonard Forster, and C.P. Magill, for Basil Blackwell in Oxford (1953).

BIOGRAPHICAL AND CRITICAL WORKS
(CHIEFLY IN ENGLISH)

Alberes, R. M., and Boisdeffre, Pierre de, *Kafka: The Torment of Man.* New York: Philosophical Library, 1968.

Anders, Gunther, *Franz Kafka.* London: Bowes and Bowes, 1960.

Arendt, Hannah, "Franz Kafka: A Revaluation," *Partisan Review*, II (Fall 1944), 412-422.

Auden, W. H., *The Dyer's Hand.* New York: Random House, 1962.

Barthes, Roland, *Critical Essays.* Translated by Richard Howard. Evanston, Illinois: Northwestern University Press, 1966.

Baumer, Franz, *Franz Kafka.* New York: Frederick Ungar, 1971.

Bauer, Johann, *Kafka and Prague.* New York: Praeger, 1971.

Beck, Evelyn, *Kafka and the Yiddish Theater.* Madison: The University of Wisconsin Press, 1971.

Belgion, Montgomery, "The Measure of Kafka," *The Criterion* (October 1938), 13-28.

Borges, Jorge Luis, *Labyrinths.* New York: New Directions, 1962.

Brod, Max, *Franz Kafka: A Biography.* New York: Schocken Books, 1960.

Buber-Neumann, Margarete, *Mistress to Kafka: The Life and Death of Milena.* Introduction by Arthur Koestler. London: Secker and Warburg, 1966.

Burgum, Edwin Berry, "Kafka on Many Levels," *Virginia Quarterly Review*, XXIV, No. 3 (Summer 1948), 464-469.

Carrouges, Michel, *Kafka versus Kafka.* University, Alabama: The University of Alabama Press, 1968.

Cohn, Dorrit, "Kafka's Eternal Present: Narrative Tense in 'Ein Landarzt' and Other First Person Stories," *PMLA*, 83 (1968), 144-150.

_____. "Castles and Anti-Castles, or Kafka and Robbe-Grillet," *Novel: A Forum on Fiction,* V, No. 1 (Spring 1971), 19-31.

Collins, Hildegard, "Kafka's Views of Institutions and Traditions," *German Quarterly*, XXXV (1962), 492-503.

Cook, Mary, *The Woman Characters in the Novels of Franz Kafka.* Columbia University, Master's Thesis, 1947.

Cuevas, Jose Luis, *The Worlds of Kafka and Cuevas.* Philadelphia: Falcon Press, 1959.

Dymant, Dora, "Ich Habe Franz Kafka Geliebt," *Die Neue Zeitung*, August 18, 1948, p. 1.

Emrich, Wilhelm, *Franz Kafka: A Critical Study of His Writing.* New York: Frederick Ungar, 1968.

Eisner, Pavel, *Franz Kafka and Prague*. New York: Golden Griffin Books, 1950.

Fickert, Kurt, J., "The Window Metaphor in Kafka's *The Trial*," *Monatshefte,* LXIII (1966), 345-352.

Flores, Angel, ed., *The Kafka Problem*. New York: New Directions, 1946.

——— and Swander, Homer, eds., *Franz Kafka Today*. Madison: University of Wisconsin Press, 1958.

Foulkes, A., *The Reluctant Pessimist: A Study of Franz Kafka*. The Hague: Mouton Press, 1967.

Fraiberg, Selma, "Kafka and the Dream," *Partisan Review*, XXIII (Winter 1956), 47-69.

Fromm, Erich, "Symbolic Language in Myth, Fairy Tales, Ritual and Novel: Kafka's *The Trial*," *The Forgotten Language*. London: Gollancz, 1952.

Frynta, Emanuel, *Kafka and Prague*. Translated by Jean Layton. London: Batchworth Press, 1960.

Glicksberg, Charles, "The Animal Image of the Self," *The Self in Modern Literature*. University Park: Pennsylvania State University Press, 1963.

Goldschmidt, H. L., "Key to Kafka," *Commentary,* VIII (August 1949), 129-138.

Goodman, Paul, *Kafka's Prayer*. New York: Vanguard, 1947.

Gordon, Caroline, "Notes on Hemingway and Kafka," *Sewanee Review*, LVII (Spring 1949), 215-226.

Gray, Ronald, *Kafka's Castle*. Cambridge: Cambridge University Press, 1956.

———. ed *Kafka: A Collection of Critical Essays*. Englewood Cliffs, New Jersey: Prentice-Hall, 1962.

Greenberg, Alvin, "Franz Kafka' by Jorge Luis Borges," *New American Review,* 8 (January 1970), 155-163.

Greenberg, Martin, *The Terror of Art: Kafka and Modern Literature*. New York: Basic Books, 1968.

Groethuysen, Bernard, "Apropos of Kafka," *Quarterly Review of Literature*, II, No. 3 (1945), 237-249.

Guth, Hans P., "Symbol and Contextual Restraint: Kafka's 'A Country Doctor,'" *PMLA,* LXXX (1965), 427-431.

Hall, Calvin, and Lind, Richard, *Dreams, Life, and Literature: A Study of Franz Kafka*. Chapel Hill: The University of North Carolina Press, 1970.

Hamalian, Leo, "Kafka in Poland," *Columbia University Forum*, IV, No. 1 (Winter 1961), 40-43.

_____. "The Great Wall of Kafka," *The Journal of Modern Literature*, I, No. 2 (1970), 254-261.

Heller, Erich, "The World of Franz Kafka," *The Disinherited Mind*. London: Bowes and Bowes, 1952.

Heller, Peter, *Dialectics and Nihilism*. Amherst: The University of Massachusetts Press, 1966.

Hoffman, Frederick, *The Mortal No*. Princeton, New Jersey: Princeton University Press, 1964.

Jaffe, Adrian, *The Process of Kafka's Trial*. East Lansing: Michigan State University Press, 1967.

Janouch, Gustav, *Conversations with Kafka*. New York: Praeger, 1953.

Jolas, Eugene, "Franz Kafka's Stories and Ascending Romanticism," *Vertical Yearbook*. New York: Gotham Book Mart, 1941.

Kauf, Robert, "Once Again—Kafka's 'Report to an Academy,'" *Modern Language Quarterly*, XV (December 1954), 359-366.

Kavanaugh, Thomas, "*The Trial* as Semiology," *Novel: A Forum for Fiction*, V, No. 3 (Spring 1972), 242-253.

Lesser, Simon, "The Source of Guilt and the Sense of Guilt: Kafka's *The Trial*," *Modern Fiction Studies*, VIII (1962), 44-60.

MacAndrew, Elizabeth, "A Splacknuck and a Dung-Beetle: Realism and Probability in Swift and Kafka," *College English*, XXXI (January 1970), 376-391.

Mann, Thomas, "Homage," *The Castle*. New York: Random House, 1954. 1954.

Margeson, John, "Franz Kafka: A Critical Problem," *University of Toronto Quarterly*, XVIII (October 1948), 30-40.

Marshall, Lee, ed., *The Trial of 6 Designers*. With an essay on *The Trial* by Kenneth Rexroth. Lock Haven, Pennsylvania: Hammermill Paper Company, 1968.

Mellen, Joan, "Joseph K. and the Law," *Texas Studies in Literature and Language*, XIII (Summer 1970), 295-302.

Muir, Edwin, trans. "Introductory Note," *The Castle*. New York: Alfred Knopf, 1930.

_____. "Introductory Note," *The Great Wall of China*, London: Secker, 1933.

"Near View of Kafka," *Mosaic*, III (Summer 1970). This special number devoted to Kafka is available from the University of Manitoba Press.

Neider, Charles, *The Frozen Sea*. New York: Oxford University Press, 1948.

Neumarkt, Paul, "Kafka's 'A Hunger Artist': The Ego in Isolation," *American Imago*, XXVII (Summer 1970), 109-121.

Neumeyer, Peter, ed., *Twentieth Century Interpretations of The Castle*. Englewood Cliffs, New Jersey: Prentice-Hall, 1969.

Osborne, Charles, *Kafka*. New York: Barnes and Noble; London: Oliver and Boyd, 1967.

Paz, Octavio, "Metamorphosis," *Alternating Current*. New York: Viking Press, 1973.

Politzer, Heinz, *Franz Kafka: Parable and Paradox*. Ithaca, New York: Cornell University Press, 1962.

Rhein, Philip H., *The Urge to Live: A Comparative Study of Franz Kafka's* Der Prozess *and Albert Camus'* L'Etranger. Chapel Hill: University of North Carolina Press, 1964.

Robert, Marthe, *Kafka*. Paris: Gallimard, 1960.

Roth, Philip, "'I Always Wanted You to Admire My Fasting'; or Looking at Kafka," *American Review*, 17 (May 1973), 103-127.

Rubenstein, William, "Franz Kafka's 'A Report to the Academy,'" *Modern Language Quarterly*, XIII (December 1952), 372-376.

Sarraute, Nathalie, "From Dostoyevsky to Kafka," *The Age of Suspicion*. New York: George Braziller, 1963.

Sartre, Jean-Paul, "'Aminadab,'" *Literary Essays*. New York: Philosophical Library, 1957.

Singer, Carl S., "Kafka's *The Trial:* The Examined Life," *Approaches to the Twentieth Century Novel*. John Unterrecker, ed. New York: Columbia University Press, 182-217.

———. *Discovery of America by Accident: A Study of Form and Value of the Novel in Kafka's Art*. Thesis, Columbia University, 1971.

Slochower, Harry, *No Voice Is Wholly Lost*. New York: Farrar, Straus, and Cudahy, 1946.

Sokel, Walter, *Franz Kafka*. New York and London: Columbia University Press, 1966.

Spilka, Mark, *Dickens and Kafka*. London: Dobson, 1963.

Spahr, Blake, "Franz Kafka: The Bridge and the Abyss," *Modern Fiction Studies*, VIII (1962), 3-15.

Stallman, Robert, "A Hunger Artist," *Accent*, No. 8 (Winter 1948). Also appears in *The Art of Modern Fiction*, New York: Holt, Rinehart and Winston, 1949.

Steinberg, Edwin R., "K. of *The Castle*: Ostensible Land-Surveyor," *College English*, XXVII, No. 3 (December 1965), 185-189.

Steiner, George, "K.," *Language and Silence*. New York: Atheneum, 1972.

Steinhaur, Harry, "Hungering Artist or Artist in Hungering: Kafka's 'A Hunger Artist,'" *Criticism*, IV (1962), 28-43.

Szanto, George, *Narrative Consciousness: Structure and Perception in the Fiction of Kafka, Beckett, and Robbe-Grillet.* Austin: University of Texas Press, 1972.

Tauber, Herbert, *Franz Kafka: An Interpretation of His Works.* New Haven: Yale University Press; London: Martin Secker and Warburg, Ltd., 1948.

Taylor, Alexander, "The Waking: The Theme of Kafka's 'Metamorphosis,'" *Studies in Short Fiction*, II (1964), 337-342.

Thomas, J. D., "The Dark at the End of the Tunnel: Kafka's 'In the Penal Colony,'" *Studies in Short Fiction* IV (1966), 12-18.

Thorlby, Anthony, *A Student's Guide to Kafka.* London: Heinemann Educational Books, Ltd., 1972.

Tiefenbrun, Ruth, *Moment of Torment.* Carbondale and Edwardsville: The University of Southern Illinois Press, 1973.

Turner, Alison, "Kafka's Two Worlds of Music," *Monatshefte*, LV (1963), 265-276.

Urdazil, Johannes, *There Goes Kafka.* Detroit, Michigan: Wayne State University, 1968.

Vivas, Eliseo, "Kafka's Distorted Mask," *Creation and Discovery.* New York: Noonday Press, 1955.

Votaw, Albert, "Kafka and Mrs. Blandish," *Horizon* (London), XX, No. 117 (September 1949), 145-160.

Warren, Austin, "Cosmos Kafka," *Rage for Order.* Chicago: University of Chicago Press, 1948.

Webster, Peter Dow, "'Dies Irae' in the Unconscious, or The Significance of Franz Kafka," *College English*, XII, No. 1 (1950), 9-15.

Weigand, Hermann J., "Franz Kafka's 'The Burrow' ('Der Bau'): An Analytical Essay," *PMLA*, Vol. 87, No. 2 (March 1972).

Weinberg, Helen, *The New Novel in America: The Kafkan Mode in Contemporary Fiction.* Ithaca, New York: Cornell University Press, 1970.

West, Rebecca, *The Court and the Castle.* New Haven: Yale University Press, 1957.

Wilson, Edmund, "A Dissenting Opinion on Kafka," *Classics and Commercials.* New York: Farrar Straus, 1950.